AUSTRALIAN SOCCER'S
LONG ROAD TO THE TOP

AUSTRALIAN SOCCER'S
LONG ROAD TO THE TOP

MICHAEL COCKERILL

To Mike Petersen,
an honest man, a quality player and ultimately, a true believer.

Cover Photograph:
Harry Kewell at the Melbourne Cricket Ground.
TONY FEDER COURTESY OF SPORTING PIX

Thomas C. Lothian Pty Ltd
11 Munro Street, Port Melbourne VIC 3207

Created and produced by
Brewster Publishers Pty Ltd
PO Box 3231, Tamarama
NSW 2026 Australia

First published 1998

Copyright © Brewster Publishers Pty Ltd 1998

All rights reserved. No part of this publication may be reproduced, stored in a retrieval system or transmitted in any form by any means without the prior permission of the copyright owner. Enquiries should be made to the publisher.

National Library of Australia Cataloguing-in-Publication Data:

Australian soccer's long road to the top.

ISBN 0 85091 892 8.

1. Socceroos (Soccer team). 2. Soccer - Australia.
I. Cockerill, Michael.

796.334660994

Printed in Sydney by Alken Press

CONTENTS

Chapter 1 El Telepathy 1

Chapter 2 The Inheritance 12

Chapter 3 Thommo's Rule 27

Chapter 4 The Talent Drain 43

Chapter 5 The Arrival 50

Chapter 6 Pompeyroos 61

Chapter 7 The Foreign Legion 69

Chapter 8 Tales from Oceania 77

Chapter 9 Taming the Kiwis 86

Chapter 10 Tension Builds 95

Chapter 11 The Big One 104

Chapter 12 Tears for Fears 121

Chapter 13 Desert Storm 129

Chapter 14 The Fab Five 138

Chapter 15 Back to Basics 151

Chapter 16 All is not Lost 157

Appendix The Matches 167

ACKNOWLEDGEMENTS

I would like to acknowledge the following: my partner, Jo, for her love, support, and belief; my children Daisy and Tobias, for being a constant source of inspiration; my father John, for fiercely upholding the integrity of the written word; my mother, Betty, for her encouragement; the Socceroo classes of 1985 and 1989, for playing for the love of their country, rather than for the love of money; my various sports editors at the *Sydney Morning Herald* for sending me away with the national team; and the late Lawrie Schwab for his excellent book, *The Socceroos and their opponents*.

CHAPTER 1

EL TELEPATHY

INSIDE THE LOUNGE AT SCRIBES, Terry Venables was wearing a cork hat and brandishing a boomerang—trying his hardest to look like an Australian. Outside on Kensington High Street, it looked anything but. Snow is a rare occurrence in London, mid-November. But so was this. Five months after he had managed England to the precipice of European Championship glory, Venables told a packed press conference that he had agreed to become the new national coach of Australia. Nineteen November 1996 would go down as the day one of the biggest names in the world's biggest sport went from the penthouse to the basement in a single dizzying slide.

Or so the next day's Fleet Street headlines went. 'I thought it was April Fool's Day when I first heard the news,' screamed former Scotland international Alan Hansen in the *Daily Express*. 'It's right up there with being manager of the Jamaican bobsleigh squad,' sneered columnist Richard Littlejohn in the *Daily Mail*. But Venables knew something the assembled hacks at his members-only club in west London did not: Australia possessed a decent soccer team. Venables was happy to back his own judgment. He was supremely confident he would be proved right in the end.

However, in the days that followed the public announcement, the priority was to ride out the storm. Twenty thousand kilometres away in Australia, the initial reaction to the appointment had been only fractionally more complimentary. Most of the angst centred on the revelation that the new national coach would not even be required to live in Australia. He would continue to reside in England. Venables was tagged 'El Telepathy', or 'Oz-Tel', with heartfelt concerns that he would end up coaching the Socceroos by remote control.

Former national captain Johnny Warren labelled it as an insult to everyone involved in the game at a domestic level. Others found it equally hard to disguise their dismay. 'Somebody is taking us for a ride,' said Marconi-Fairfield coach Manfred Schaefer. 'I think it's a slap in the face for all the local coaches who have worked so hard to put Australia on the map,' complained Adelaide City coach John Nyskohus.

But Venables, and the man who had steered him into the job, Soccer Australia chairman David Hill, were never likely to take much notice of such strident criticism. True enough, they may have been disappointed, perhaps even mildly surprised, that the appointment had not met with universal acclaim. But the furore only served to increase their determination. Two strong, wilful characters had made a pact. This was going to work. They would make certain of it.

For Venables, it was a landmark decision in a long and eventful career. There had been other opportunities on his plate, including a lucrative offer from Blackburn Rovers and another from the Egyptian national team. But they represented a safer, more familiar course. Venables knew all about working within the highest echelons of the game—big clubs, big names, big money. But Australia offered a completely different kind of challenge: to take charge of a team which, at that point, was ranked no. 52 in the world and guide them to the World Cup finals. Having recently departed the international stage with some regret, he was enthusiastic about the chance to make a quick return. And if England fancied their chances of qualifying for France 98, so did Australia. Venables took the scorn in his stride. Beneath the smiling veneer lurked a backbone of steel. The risk may have been all his, but he had done his calculations. He never doubted that he had made a smart choice.

Venables, certainly, was quick to appreciate that Australia possessed a team of genuine potential. The problem was that under the guidance of former national coach Eddie Thomson they had not often been given the encouragement to exploit it. But Thomson was gone, having been released from the final 18 months of his contract to accept a lucrative offer from Japanese club Sanfrecce Hiroshima. Although Venables would start with just 18 months lead-in time to the World Cup finals, he effectively represented the chance to start with a clean slate.

That, certainly, was uppermost in the mind of Hill, who had had his share of

E/L T/E/L/E/P/A/T/H/Y

disagreements with Thomson towards the end of the coach's reign. Most famously, there had been a blazing row just months before, when Hill had stormed into the Socceroo dressing-room in Johannesburg after the team had been beaten 2–0 by South Africa in the Simba Cup tournament. Hill was especially displeased with the dismissal of defender Tony Popovic, and at the dressing-room door—well, within earshot of the players—he accused Thomson of, among other things, failing to instil enough discipline in his team. Thomson replied angrily, telling Hill in the plainest terms that he might be better off doing the job himself.

In fact, there was something important Hill didn't know at the time. Just a few days previously, Thomson had met with officials of Sanfrecce in Durban, where the Socceroos had beaten Ghana 2–0 in their opening game of the South African tournament. In truth, the coach was already halfway out the door.

The two men patched up their differences, but after returning to Australia the following weekend, Hill first learnt of the rumours connecting Thomson to a job in Japan. 'I asked him straight out, but he denied it,' said Hill.

A week later, the story broke in the *Sydney Morning Herald*. Thomson again denied everything, this time in print. But within 24 hours, his declaration of innocence had collapsed in a heap. Sanfrecce officials told the *Herald* that Thomson had been offered a two-year contract worth $500 000 per year, and that he was due in Hiroshima the following week to finalise the deal. Thomson was hauled in before Hill and Soccer Australia chief executive David Woolley, and for the first time he conceded that he had, indeed, been approached.

In the meantime, there was some unfinished business to attend to. That week the Socceroos were to play a friendly international against Saudi Arabia in Riyadh— a game that had been arranged at short notice. As it turned out, this was to be Thomson's swan song. Fittingly for a coach who had become bogged down in dour, negative tactics, he signed off with a scoreless draw. Thomson then flew direct from Riyadh to Hiroshima, about the same time the board met in Adelaide to discuss his future. 'I wasn't happy that we didn't really know what was going on, and I made it clear I felt he should go,' said board member George Negus. The board's prevailing mood was communicated to Thomson. Not surprisingly, after a brief deliberation with officials of Sanfrecce he agreed to join the J League.

On Wednesday, 16 October 1996, Thomson jetted back into Sydney and went immediately to the offices of Soccer Australia to hand in his resignation. It was, he said the following day, 'the hardest decision of my life'.

But it wasn't such a hard decision for others to accept. Thomson insisted he left the Socceroos in better shape than he inherited them, but the statistics suggested otherwise: a win ratio of less than 50 per cent over seven years, a record of barely a goal per game, and hardly any results of substance against strong opposition. It is true that the quality of Australian players had risen dramatically during his time, but clearly someone other than Thomson would be needed to convert that potential into meaningful results. The question, of course, was who?

The answer to that question lay in the hands of Soccer Australia, and in particular, Hill. For the short term, at least, long-serving national staff coach Raul Blanco was to be given control of the Socceroos on a caretaker basis. Although widely respected within the game, he had only six months before accepted a full-time position as head coach of the national under-23 team for the Sydney 2000 Olympics. Blanco kept his hat in the ring for the Socceroo job, and was publicly anointed by Thomson at his farewell press conference. But in the circumstances, few believed he would get the job on a permanent basis—unless he stepped aside as Olympic coach. Which he wasn't inclined to do.

Blanco, nonetheless, did get to take the Socceroos into the Oceania Nations Cup final against Tahiti, to be played home and away in early November. As a result, history will remember him as the most successful national coach in history. A 6–0 win in Papeete and a 5–0 win in Canberra on the return leg left Blanco with a record to be envied. But although he had many backers, such results against patently inferior opposition were never likely to count towards his claims for the top job in the game.

On the morning after the Tahiti match at Bruce Stadium, the board of Soccer Australia met again in a Canberra hotel, this time to discuss the vacant coaching position. By this stage, a host of names were being bandied about in the media, virtually all of them based locally. The feeling was that with the World Cup qualifiers just six months away, it would be too risky to go with a coach who had little inside knowledge of the Australian game.

Heading the list of contenders was the taciturn Zoran Matic. Not only had he won three championships with Adelaide City, he had provided the backbone of the Socceroo team throughout the Thomson era. And at the same time as the vacancy was being discussed by the board, Matic had taken his Collingwood Warriors team to the pre-season title and an early lead in the national league. Impeccable timing, indeed.

Other credible candidates included one-time Socceroo teammates John Kosmina, David Ratcliffe and Frank Farina, and Sydney United's urbane coach, Branko

E/L T/E/L/E/P/A/T/H/Y

Culina. The former head coach of the Australian Institute of Sport, Ron Smith, was also promoted as an alternative. The majority of Socceroo players had been through the AIS while Smith was in charge, and he had enhanced his case by making a huge success of his first overseas appointment with Sabah in the Malaysian league.

The overwhelming feeling within the board of Soccer Australia, at that point, was to go with a local appointment. But as the commissioners met in Canberra, Hill was contemplating alternatives.

'We didn't take a vote. We were basically trying to assess what the mood was,' he said. 'I wanted it to be a football decision, and I wanted it to be unanimous. There was some vagueness historically about how Sir Arthur George [the former chairman] had unilaterally appointed Rudi Gutendorf, so I thought it was important that it was a unanimous decision if we could get it.

'There was more support for Matic than anybody else, partly because there was a real South Australian influence at the time. There was support for Raul Blanco as well. Certainly the mood was for a local appointment. But in my opinion, nobody had lifted their sights. Nobody had even thought about looking overseas.'

This was not entirely true. One of the reasons Hill's old ABC mate Negus had been enticed to join the board of Soccer Australia was the persuasion applied by Craig Johnston, the former Liverpool midfielder who throughout the 1980s was easily the country's most recognisable player. Johnston may never have played for the Socceroos, and may have infamously stated that playing soccer for Australia was 'like surfing for England', but he did keep a watching brief on the state of the game. A year earlier, Johnston had publicly floated the idea of the national team being guided by a British coach. It was something he and Negus had often discussed. So when Thomson departed, Johnston was on the phone again, this time with a list of potential candidates. That list was forwarded to Hill.

Johnston had already done some of the groundwork. He had just become involved in a six-a-side tournament called World Series, which kicked off in early 1997 with some of Europe's leading clubs—among them Glasgow Rangers, Liverpool and Ajax—contesting the inaugural competition at the new Amsterdam Arena. Venables was also involved in the organisation of World Series, as was Johann Cruyff.

Johnston had initially alerted Venables to the potential of Australian soccer when they had met at England's headquarters at Bisham Abbey during the build-up to Euro 96. He subsequently admired his work during this tournament, in which England were unlucky not to have made the final at Germany's expense.

'I'd rate him as one of the top five coaches in the world,' says Johnston. 'When I rang him after Euro 96 to ask him if he was interested in the Socceroo job, he just chuckled and said, "Are you serious?" We had a good chat about things. He thought it was disgraceful the way he had been treated by the English FA, and in the end he started to come around.'

Hill, meantime, was starting to move at the Australian end. 'I had begun to make communications overseas. I told the board what I was doing, although I didn't name anybody in particular. Basically, I only consulted with Basil Scarsella [the vice-chairman]. We thought about the top coaches who were available, and we narrowed it down to a list of three.'

An impressive list it was, too: Cruyff, recently resigned as manager of Barcelona FC and widely acclaimed as one of the best players the world had seen; Venables, recently departed as manager of England; and Kenny Dalglish, arguably the most successful manager in the English game but at that stage 'between jobs' after leaving Blackburn Rovers.

Cruyff, the autocratic Dutchman, had the early running. Says Hill: 'We had already started to check his availability through his manager, Jaap de Groot. We were in regular contact with him, and Cruyff knew we were interested. Things looked fairly promising, I'd say.'

But Hill, born in England and a self-confessed Anglophile, had his personal favourite. It was the same name that had been on top of Johnston's list. Venables. The fact that it seemed such a long shot to recruit the former England manager only served to intensify Hill's fascination. For a man not averse to self-aggrandisement, this was a coup he wanted desperately to pull off.

As a coup, though, it had humble beginnings. Just how Hill initially manoeuvred himself into Venables' inner sanctum remains a story in itself. The intermediary was not a manager or an agent, according to the chairman. In fact it was a humble office girl—Tina.

'She was a temp on a working holiday, and she was working with Soccer Australia,' said Hill. 'She used to work with the Football Association [FA]. On the first floor where the coaches are, it's like an old gentlemen's club. It's a very regimented office, "toffy-nosed" is how Tina described it. But they had real workers as stenographers. When I took her aside and asked her if she had ever met Venables, she said she had, many times. She really liked him. So I said, "Can you try to get hold of him please?" Apparently all the girls would go to Scribes on their nights out, and that's where she ended up making the contact. The word came back that, yes, he was prepared to talk.'

And so the chase was on. Venables had emerged, in Hill's mind, as the clear target. But discussions with de Groot were also progressing well, with Cruyff on holiday in California at the time. Another candidate also emerged, with contacts in Australia recommending Howard Wilkinson, recently sacked as manager of Leeds United. Although the feelers were out for Dalglish, he never gave Soccer Australia the impression he was genuinely interested.

Jack Charlton's name also popped up. The hugely successful manager of the Republic of Ireland had relatives in Australia, and was available, having just quit his post after eight memorable years. But the long-ball style which had been fundamental to the Irish game-plan concerned Hill and his confidant, Scarsella.

'We didn't consult widely on it, to be fair, but we couldn't detect any great enthusiasm at this end for Charlton despite the terrific things he did for Ireland,' said Hill. 'We made the assessment that it wouldn't work.'

Hill's intuition kept telling him that Venables was the man for the moment. But after the initial contact, things had slowed down from the London end. Venables had requested an information kit on the Socceroos, and Hill—in the interests of secrecy—had sent him the details by fax from his home in Randwick. The information kit included details of recent Australian performances and a brief outline on the talent that was available to the national team. In reply, Hill heard… nothing.

'In our first conversation he had been guarded, and I didn't want to pressure him,' said Hill. 'But a week went by and I didn't hear a word. I got a bit concerned. Usually you have a sense about these things, and I thought that was it. So I got hold of Tina again and said, "I don't want to bug you, but can you find out if he's interested so we can close the door on it." She was staying in a flat in Redfern, and we had to drop off a mobile so she could contact Venables out of business hours. She rang me and said he wanted to talk some more.'

It was time, Hill decided, to push things along. The preferred choices had been narrowed to Venables or Cruyff, but Hill had still to talk directly to the Dutchman. Now he wanted to up the ante. The decision was made to fly to Europe to attempt to finalise the appointment. Venables implored Hill and Scarsella not to come purely on his account, but they were not to be dissuaded.

Hill not only believed in his powers of persuasion, he was convinced that what he was offering was a very attractive job. Money aside, the Australian post had a lot going for it; a good team, with good players, with good fortune having decreed the easiest World Cup qualifying route of any nation on Earth. It was just a question of pushing the point, that was all.

On 13 November, a month after Thomson had handed in his resignation, Hill and Scarsella flew out of Sydney on Swissair, bound for Zurich and then London. Before the coaching appointment could be finalised, they were keen to know more about the most important factor—money. Hill had an idea of how far Soccer Australia's finances could be stretched, but he still wasn't sure if it would be enough to get their man. One person who did have an understanding of the likely asking rate was Sepp Blatter, the general secretary of the Federation Internationale de Football Association (FIFA). Blatter's daughter, Corinne, worked for Soccer Australia, and he had a soft spot for the country. There were other pertinent matters to discuss during the stopover in Zurich, but Hill was hoping Blatter would help him out on the coaching position. He did.

What Blatter told the Soccer Australia delegation only confirmed Hill's belief that Venables—if not Cruyff—was within his price range. He had also done some homework elsewhere. It remains a little known fact that Australia has, by rights, a representative on the board of the Football Association; a throwback to colonial times, no doubt. But this quirk of history was known to Hill. Which was why he contacted his near-namesake, David Hill-Wood, and put him on the spot: find out how much Terry was on for the England job, will you? 'It was probably information we shouldn't have had,' said Hill, 'but he gave it to us, and it was extremely helpful in the end.'

After spending a few hours with Blatter in Zurich, Hill and Scarsella knew the ballpark figure. They also had a crucial piece of inside information. They were, therefore, forewarned and forearmed when they flew into Heathrow for their meeting with Venables at Scribes. What they knew as fact was that as manager of England—one of the biggest jobs in world football—Venables had been paid an annual salary of £175 000 plus bonuses. Hill was prepared to match that, and perhaps even throw in a little bit more.

But money, as Hill recalls, never became the core issue. After an introduction and a brief chat at Scribes, the three men walked to the nearby Royal Garden Hotel, which enjoys a sweeping view of Kensington Park Gardens. Upstairs, over a coffee and biscuits, they got down to the business of bargaining.

According to Hill: 'He was still very non-committal, so I jumped in and said bang, bang, bang, here it is. Interestingly enough, he didn't haggle about money at all. We started at $350 000 and ended up $400 000. Done. What he really wanted was to satisfy himself that he wanted the job in his heart of hearts. He didn't want to be hurried or harried. He said, "How long have I got?" We said, "As long as you like", which of course was a lie. This was a Wednesday, and Basil had to go back home on the Saturday. I had a lot to do as well. But I knew that for him, having some time to mull things over was an important consideration. So I was prepared to wait.'

But Venables was smart enough to establish one important prerequisite. For a job that would involve many hours of travel, he wanted to be able to fly first class. On the way back from the Royal Garden Hotel to Scribes, he played the detective role every bit as well as the celebrated Hazell character he had dreamed up for the television series of the same name years before.

'We're walking down Kensington High Street, basically talking small talk,' recalled Hill. 'Terry turns around and says, "How was the flight? Did you travel first class?" Basil says yes, but the truth is we had been upgraded. I turned around and said, "You've buggered that, Basil. I mean we can hardly negotiate business class for Terry when we've just admitted we travelled first class to get here." It was the one concession we ended up making in the negotiations.'

Back at Scribes, over a sumptuous Spanish meal at the club restaurant, the three men gradually warmed to each other. With the fundamental issue of money having been overcome, the mood became relaxed and cheerful. Yvette, Venables' wife, introduced herself briefly at the start of lunch and later joined the men for coffee and desserts.

'You can never be sure, because Terry is a businessman, after all,' said Hill, 'but when Yvette joined us at the table I got a feeling that the deal was done.' It was, but not just yet.

That evening a jet-lagged Hill and Scarsella sat in the new North Bank stand at Highbury to watch Arsenal and Stoke City do battle in the League Cup. Venables spent the night discussing the job with his wife and his advisers. Another meeting was scheduled for Scribes in the morning, but Hill decided to jump the gun. He phoned a long-time friend back in Sydney, Zeke Solomon, who was a senior partner in the law firm Allen, Allen and Hemsley. He wanted the firm's London office to help him draw up an employment contract, even though agreement had not yet been reached.

After more discussions with Venables, largely centred around contract conditions, the would-be Socceroo coach left for club duties at Portsmouth, where his role at the time was as technical director. His prospective employers spent the afternoon and evening drafting a contract. Cruyff, by this stage, had been eliminated from the equation. 'Culturally and linguistically I had always felt Venables would be closer to the Australian idiom than Cruyff,' said Hill. 'There is a connection between an East End Londoner and an Australian. Terry later described us as a classless society. There was certainly a lack of reserve, a warmth, an affinity between Terry and Yvette and us. I think he was getting increasingly comfortable with the idea. He had always been the lower order employed by the higher order. I think he enjoyed being a social equal. He finds Australians very refreshing like that.'

There were further discussions with the lawyers the following day, when Venables was tied up with other business. But Hill did take time out to meet Howard Wilkinson at his hotel near Marble Arch. The ex-manager of Leeds United was, in Hill's words, 'keen as mustard' for the Australian position. But in truth, Wilkinson was never considered a serious candidate.

Things had come to a head. Early on the Saturday morning, before another meeting was scheduled with Venables, Hill and Scarsella contacted all of their fellow board members to get a vote on the impending appointment. That afternoon Venables was due to go to Portsmouth to watch his team play, while Hill and Scarsella had been given tickets by Venables to watch Tottenham host Sunderland at White Hart Lane. Before they went their separate ways, Hill wanted to be sure the board of Soccer Australia was fully behind the decision.

President Neville Wran, the former premier of New South Wales, was contacted early in the morning in a hotel room in Vienna. 'You just make sure you tell Terry I'm freezing my balls off for him,' he croaked to Hill over the phone. Negus was found in the airport lounge in Munich, on his way to shooting a story for 'Foreign Correspondent'. Sue Baker-Finch was contacted at home in Canberra, Peter Gray was found in the airport bar at Adelaide, Don di Fabrizio was in Perth on business, and Fred Lenzi was contacted at a restaurant in Adelaide.

Lenzi was later to express some reservations after being faxed a summary of the contract, but what mattered most to Hill was that, officially, he had gained the board's full support. 'The vote was unanimous, and the minutes record it as such,' he said.

Scarsella flew out of London that night confident the deal had been sealed. Although the contract was now into its third draft, and the negotiations were proceeding 'without prejudice', there seemed no more obstacles to be overcome. The next morning Venables admitted as much, telling the public in his weekly column in the *News of the World* that he was '99 per cent sure' of taking the Australian job. A few hours later, in the boutique Mile End Hotel in Kensington, he proved true to his word. Venables offered his hand to Hill, and the deal was done.

A final contract was drawn up between lawyers representing both sides the following day, while Hill took time out to visit a niece in Oxford and to try to find a rare copy of the diaries of the minister for foreign affairs in Mussolini's wartime Italian government. His luck was in. 'It was almost as good as signing Venables,' said Hill.

The signing, it had been agreed, would be held with appropriate pomp and ceremony before the television cameras at Scribes the next day. Hill shared a cab on the way to the conference with Soccer Australia's London-based agent, Michael Darcy. Outside it was snowing heavily, but inside Hill was feeling warm as toast. Darcy turned to him and said in his best cockney twang, 'I didn't believe you could get him. Us Londoners don't like to travel. If we go outside the M25 [London's ring road] we get a nose bleed.'

Hill laughed. He was feeling pretty content with himself. Everyone had said it couldn't be done, but he had got his man in the end.

Johnston, too, was elated when the news was confirmed. 'I'm pleased I was able to put something back into Australian soccer, in my own way,' he says. 'I didn't do it as a player, and I'm sorry about that. But I'm proud that this worked out. It was all about lifting the standard of thinking. From a player's perspective. From the media perspective. From a coaching perspective. The purpose was to take Australian soccer to a new threshold.'

CHAPTER 2

THE INHERITANCE

SO WHAT EXACTLY DID TERRY VENABLES inherit when he agreed, amid much fanfare, to take on the job of coaching Australia? According to a former national coach, Frank Arok, he stepped into a 'ready-made situation'. 'There was an incredible richness of players around the place,' said Arok. 'We could have put together two and a half teams and not known which was the best one.'

It was hard to disagree. But it was not just the here and now which made the Australian post so attractive. There was an overpowering sense of destiny surrounding the national team. The feeling was that only a travesty of justice would deny the Socceroos their rightful place in the World Cup finals.

That Venables was able to inherit arguably the best generation of Australian talent in history was no accident. Three decades of selfless, unpaid and unheralded work by various players, coaches and administrators had planted the seed. The earth was as fertile as it had ever been. While the sport in Australia may have wasted many opportunities in its chequered history, the national team, the Socceroos, boasted a strong, proud tradition: to never say die, to refuse to be intimidated, to ignore the odds. Venables sensed this special atmosphere almost immediately. He respected it and identified with it. He harvested it. But it was others who had laid the groundwork. And they deserve to be remembered for it.

It was a Sydney journalist, Tony Horsted, who had coined the term 'Socceroos' for the national team thirty years before. In 1967 the team, under coach Joe Vlasits, took the nickname away with it on a tour to Vietnam—a tour arranged at the

THE INHERITANCE

height of the Vietnam War and with the country under siege from a Viet Cong guerilla campaign. Upon arrival at Saigon Airport, the Australians were given a briefing by security personnel and told to stay away from Americans as they represented a target for the guerillas. The players were also told not to kick sticks or stones lying on the footpath as they could be disguised bombs. With the front only 30 kilometres to the west, it was no surprise that the sound of machine-guns and mortar shells could be heard every night of the team's stay at the decrepit Golden Building hotel. But the players ignored the trying conditions to march undefeated through the National Day tournament, eventually triumphing 3–1 in the final against South Korea. A crowd of 35 000 at the Cong Hoa Stadium chanted '*Uc-Dai-Loi* [Australia] no. 1' as the Australians completed a lap of honour in ankle-deep slush. At the end of a tour in which the Australians won 10 games in a row, it was here that the Socceroo legend was born.

Two years before the Vietnam tour, Australia had entered the World Cup for the first time, but it had proved to be a short-lived and somewhat embarrassing campaign. In sharp contrast to the marathons that were to follow, Australia had to play only two games to qualify for the 1996 finals in England. FIFA drew up six African groups and one Asia–Oceania group for a series of matches to produce the 16th and final qualifier for England. However 15 African nations and South Korea withdrew their applications in protest at the inclusion of South Africa—then on the threshold of a long and painful isolation because of its racist apartheid policies. As a result only two countries were left in the draw: Australia and communist North Korea. The two matches were scheduled for the Stade Olympique in neutral Phnom Penh, Cambodia, in late November 1965. They were matches the Australians were never likely to win. While the North Koreans had played 35 internationals over three years to prepare for the World Cup qualifiers, Australia had had to be content with irregular matches against touring European club sides as preparation. The play-offs loomed as a mismatch, and they were. The outclassed and out-thought Australians, coached by Tiko Jelisvacic, were thrashed 6–1 in the first match and 3–1 in the return held three days later. Australia's first-ever World Cup match attracted 60 000 fans—the largest crowd the players had seen. The consolation goal came after 70 minutes from the penalty spot, and was scored by Les Scheinflug. (Thirty years later Scheinflug was still around to assist Venables when he took charge.) And it was Scheinflug who again scored Australia's only goal in the second match, played before another big crowd of 55 000.

The North Koreans were left to celebrate, while Australia could only return home to reflect on how much work had to be done if they were to realise their aim of playing in the finals of the World Cup. But at least it was a start. And North Korea proved to be no pushovers in England a year later, eliminating Italy in one of the biggest upsets the world had ever seen.

Indeed, considering that Australia had only just emerged from a three-year ban from international football—caused by the failure of several local clubs to pay transfer fees for imported players—the first campaign of 1965 should not be judged too harshly. In the circumstances, it was probably about as much as could have been expected.

Much more, however, was expected when the national team, under the guidance of 'Uncle Joe', approached their campaign for the World Cup in Mexico four years later; not least because some promising young Australian-born talent had emerged in the interim. The likes of Johnny Warren, Ray Baartz, Ron Corry and Billy Vojtek had all learnt their football in Australia, and were ready to challenge the imported players for a green and gold shirt. Vlasits was the first national coach to genuinely encourage and nurture local talent, at a time when naturalised citizens from Britain and Eastern Europe dominated Australian selections. It was a commendable, and visionary, policy and Vlasits would never regret looking within the horizon.

But the 1969 campaign was to end in bitter disappointment, nonetheless. The Socceroos went so close to qualifying for the finals in Mexico, only to be denied at the final hurdle. And no wonder. By the time Australia fell to Israel in the decisive qualifier, they had been forced to play nine games in four continents, with only the last match at home. In an exhausting schedule which lasted two months and cost a number of players their jobs, the Socceroos first went to Seoul, South Korea, where they triumphed over the host nation and Japan in a round-robin tournament. Having successfully negotiated that difficult hurdle, the team was 'rewarded' with a play-off against Rhodesia in neutral Laurenco Marques, Mozambique. The first two matches ended in draws, but the Australians held their nerve and their stamina to emerge victorious 3–1 in the third, and decisive, match. Incredibly, it was still not enough. FIFA decreed that the Australians would have to play two more matches to qualify for Mexico—against Israel home and away.

The Socceroos flew from Mozambique to Tel Aviv, but not directly. The journey went via Johannesburg, Luanda, Lisbon, Rome and Athens, and took 36 hours. With the kick-off scheduled for just 20 hours after their arrival, it was no surprise the Socceroos were weary from the travel and the long period away from home.

THE INHERITANCE

Two key players, defender Alan Marnoch and midfielder Danny Walsh, had been injured in the final game against Rhodesia and were sidelined for the match at the Ramat Gan Stadium. An own goal from David Zeman was enough to give the Israelis victory, even though Socceroo goalkeeper Ron Corry distinguished himself by saving a penalty. The Socceroos returned to Sydney still believing they could overcome the deficit, and a boisterous crowd of 30 000 packed the old Sydney Sportsground to see if they could do it. Sadly, the Israelis held on for a 1-1 draw, and the World Cup dream was over once again. But this time, the right foundations had been laid.

The game, generally, was developing along promising lines. Although the big crowds of the 1960s had begun to show signs of diminishing, standards on the pitch were better than they had ever been. The mass migrations of the previous two decades had left Australian soccer with a solid base of players from diverse cultures and many nationalities. These 'new' Australians, heavily influenced the home-grown players, gradually weaning them off the long-ball British style which had become their forte. It would take time, certainly, but as the Socceroos looked forward to their next World Cup campaign in 1973 the makings of a strong, skilful side were there. Arok's club side, St George, was to provide the backbone of the 1973 national team, and there was no stronger advocate of this potpourri of styles and influences. 'We had, and still have, the best cocktail of players in the world,' Arok says. Arok himself was the perfect example. Born in Novi Sad, Yugoslavia, of Hungarian parentage, he first came to Australia in the late 1960s and despite returning to Yugoslavia at semi-regular intervals, he has learned to love this country as his own. His passion for the game in Australia has remained as fervent as it was three decades ago. And his own contribution has been immense.

Yet it was not Arok but another imported Yugoslav coach who was handed the job of guiding the Socceroos to the World Cup finals of 1974. Rale Rasic took over in late 1970, when it was said he was too young and inexperienced for such an important responsibility. But Rasic, at that point the state coach of Victoria, had boundless enthusiasm and an overwhelming sense of self-belief. They were qualities that were to bring him joy and pain in equal measures. Rasic was a smart tactician, too, although his style of defence and counterattack often frustrated players and public alike. But the pattern was developing, and by the time the Socceroos were ready to open their qualifying campaign against trans-Tasman rivals New Zealand, the team looked to be in good shape.

The Kiwis provided a fright nonetheless. In the opening qualifier in Auckland, only a late goal from substitute Ernie Campbell spared Australia's blushes after the home side had gone ahead from a penalty converted by Brian Turner. It was the wake-up call the Australians needed as they prepared for their next match against Iraq in Sydney. The Iraqis and Indonesia had also been included in the so-called Asia/Oceania group. Unlike four years previously, however, the Socceroos had the benefit of playing all their early matches at home. A 3–1 win over Iraq at the Sydney Sportsground restored Australia's pride and fortunes, and it was a victory which was to prove crucial in the end. The Socceroos ultimately won the group by a single point from Iraq. New Zealand brought up the rear, despite holding the Socceroos to another draw in their return encounter in Sydney. Midfield strongman Ray Richards won the award for player of the tournament, and collected the princely sum of $100 for his efforts.

The next step for the Socceroos in their quest to reach the finals in Germany involved a play-off against Iran, who had emerged as the best team in the Asian sub-group B2. The matches were scheduled for home and away, with the opening game set down for the Sydney Sportsground. A jam-packed crowd of 30 881 watched with pride as Australia won the game 3–0 against an Iranian team which failed abysmally to live up to its reputation. An injury which had sidelined key midfielder Ali Parvin—picked up during a friendly match in New Zealand en route to Sydney—cost Iran dearly, and the Socceroos were too sharp, too committed and too good—despite playing below their potential. 'If you can win 3–0 with so many players below form you must be doing well,' said Rasic after the match. Goals from Adrian Alston and Peter Wilson set the scene, and striker Atti Abonyi capped a marvellous individual display with a tidy goal just five seconds after half-time.

The three-goal cushion seemed comfortable enough for Australia to take to the return leg in Tehran, but as events unfolded they needed every bit of it. A noisy, intimidating crowd of 80 000 awaited the Socceroos on a hot night at the newly opened Aryamehr Stadium, built just months earlier by the Shah. At a ground which the Socceroos would visit again in future campaigns, the fanatical home supporters almost succeeded in willing Iran to a miraculous comeback. Inspired by Parvis Ghelichkhani, who scored twice within the first 30 minutes, the Iranians looked certain to find the third goal which would, at the very least, force the tie into a third match. But the Socceroos dug deep, regathered their morale thanks to some herculean defence, and somehow survived the onslaught. Rarely has a defeated Australian team been so relieved to hear the final whistle. 'We pulled ourselves off

THE INHERITANCE

the floor, regained our composure and finished the game on top of Iran,' said Rasic. 'This is a sign of a team that has reached maturity.'

That much was true. But the Socceroos would be put to the test once again before they could secure their coveted place among the elite. Eight games gone, two more to go. The final of the Asia/Oceania section pitted the Socceroos against a familiar rival, South Korea. To the victor, the holy grail of a place among the 16 best nations in the world in Germany the following year; to the vanquished, the emptiness of coming so close. After two failed campaigns, the Socceroos had everything to lose and everything to play for. Having battled their way through another difficult campaign, the players—including a number of survivors from 1969—were determined not to let it slip this time. But they were in for a fight. The feeling among the Australians was that the Koreans would be easier opponents than the recently vanquished Iran. Israel, their nemesis from four years before, had been eliminated by the Koreans, and the Socceroos went into the first leg of the play-offs in Sydney believing their opponents had done them a favour. But they should have been warned—any team that had proved too good for the powerful Israelis was sure to be a useful side themselves. Which, of course, is exactly how things panned out. It needed three epic ties to resolve the issue, and in the process the Australians learnt to respect not only the Koreans but Asian football in general. Any lingering, mistaken belief in Anglo-Saxon supremacy was dispelled—once and for all.

The first match was played at the end of October, out of season for the Australian players—and it showed. But for some fine goalkeeping from Jim Fraser, just returning to the side after recovering from a back injury, the Socceroos may have been out of the tie there and then. But Australia hung on for a scoreless draw. 'The Koreans were much, much better than I had expected,' conceded Rasic. Two weeks later a more focused Socceroo side flew to Seoul for the return leg, now acutely aware of the danger posed by players such as Chung Kyu Poong and Kim Jae Han. It was, in fact, the latter who opened the scoring for the home side at the Municipal Stadium, and ten minutes later South Korea extended their lead to send the 32 000 crowd into raptures. As in Tehran a few months before, the Socceroos had left themselves badly exposed in the first half and paid a heavy price for their generosity. But, as in Tehran, they had enough composure to recover their poise and purpose. As the Koreans tired, the Socceroos found new legs, with pocket-sized midfielder Jimmy Rooney leading the fightback. A goal before the break from Branko Buljevic restored Australia's hopes, and shortly after the interval the visitors drew level when

Ray Baartz hammered the ball home after a trademark long throw from Richards. Somehow the Socceroos had clawed their way back from a two-goal deficit to draw level, but they couldn't find the vital third goal. Nonetheless, the comeback left the team in a confident mood for the tie-breaker scheduled for neutral Hong Kong a week later. 'The Koreans were finished in the second half,' said Baartz. Prophetic words, indeed. Seventy minutes into the third and deciding match, Scots-born Jimmy Mackay scored the goal of a lifetime to end the stubborn Korean resistance and send Australia into the World Cup finals for the first, and so far only, time.

Mackay, understandably, was still able to recall the defining moment with startling clarity many years later. 'Ray Richards won a free kick, Jimmy Rooney stuck the ball out to me and I hit it from about thirty yards. It was the best goal of my career.' Nobody was prepared to argue. 'I feel as though I'm walking on a cloud. I keep pinching myself to make sure the whole thing is real,' said Peter Wilson moments after the whistle. 'We kept battling our way through match after match, hoping the gods would be kind to us,' said Baartz. 'Thank heavens they were.'

It was not just the players who celebrated. A nation rejoiced, for Australia loves nothing more than a winner. This motley collection of part-timers had succeeded in etching itself forever into the game's folklore. Here was a juncture when soccer seemed certain to challenge the established sports of rugby, cricket and Australian football for pride of place in the public consciousness. The world game seemed certain to conquer one of its last frontiers as the Socceroos rode the crest of a wave of patriotic support into the 1974 World Cup finals in Germany. As a coach, Rasic vied with the likes of Jack Gibson (rugby league) and Ron Barassi (Australian football) for profile and prestige. Players such as Warren, Alston and Schaefer became stars in their own right. In the aftermath of that momentous match in Hong Kong, soccer grabbed the attention of a sports-mad nation. With a blend of British industry, Slavic skill and home-grown enthusiasm, all things seemed possible for the Socceroos, despite the ill-founded warnings of Dutchman Arie van Gemert, who had refereed the decisive match against South Korea in Hong Kong. He said: 'Australia is at least four classes lower than the weakest first division team in Europe, but Australia will play in the World Cup finals and England will not.'

Seven months later, the Socceroos arrived in Germany determined to prove the doubters, of which there were many in international football, wrong. While they succeeded in this quest, the nagging doubt remains even now that if Rasic had believed more in his players, had given them more encouragement to express their

THE INHERITANCE

skills, they may have surpassed their respectable achievements. Drawn with East Germany, West Germany and Chile, the Socceroos were desperately unfortunate to be included in such a formidable group. But a 2–0 loss to the East Germans in their opening match at least served notice that the Socceroos were much better than a condescending public and press believed. The next day's headlines told the true story. 'Dwarf grows ten feet tall.' 'Unbelievable how these Australians fight.' 'East Germany narrowly avoids disgrace.' A few days later, the Australians met the home side, West Germany, with German-born defender Schaefer the subject of much interest. But it was his partner at the back, Wilson, who left German striker Gerd Muller with lasting memories. 'He is the roughest man I've played against. He didn't seem to care whether he kicked the ball, a leg, or a head.'

Over-exuberance notwithstanding, it was the Socceroos who were cheered off the pitch by a full house at the Olympic Stadium in Munich. Despite the 3–0 defeat, they earned the admiration of the German public for their courageous display against a team which included such luminaries as Franz Beckenbauer, Sepp Maier, Muller and Gunter Netzer. The German fans would come to fully appreciate their own team when Beckenbauer lifted the World Cup three weeks later. For the beaten Australians, however, the immediate outlook was much more modest. Having succumbed to respectable defeats against the two Germanys, the target was to get a result in their final group match against Chile. This they ultimately achieved, although the Socceroos failed to score the goal the public at home had been desperately craving. Abonyi came close, but the ball stuck in the mud as he lined up his shot. The match ended in a scoreless draw, and was marred by the dismissal of the combative Richards. Nonetheless, the Socceroos were not going home empty-handed—they had hung on and managed to earn a point in their first World Cup finals.

Two decades later, it remains the only point Australia has ever gained. Nobody knew it then, but the efforts of the 1974 Socceroos would be magnified every time subsequent teams failed to measure up. The enduring shame is that an atmosphere of ill-will developed between the team and its administration before the dust had even settled. Rasic resigned shortly after the finals, but then changed his mind and reapplied. He was overlooked twice in the following three years, and his row with Soccer Australia supremo Sir Arthur George grew to overshadow all else.

The players, too, fell out with the administration over the failure to properly acknowledge their success—success which had come at a high personal cost in terms of employment and physical sacrifice. There were no medals, no receptions, there was scant public recognition of any kind. It was only midway through 1997, at a function hosted by the Port Kembla Soccer Club in Wollongong, that the team was reunited for the first time. Soccer Australia was not invited or wanted. But the national body did take the hint, and a cavalcade for the 1974 players was organised before Venables and his team took the pitch for the deciding World Cup qualifier at the Melbourne Cricket Ground against Iran. The response from the 85 000 fans that night told the real story of public appreciation for the team which had done so much to put Australian soccer on the world map. But it was an appreciation that had been denied for too long, and after more than two decades there remains a smouldering resentment among the most successful generation of Australian players.

Before and since, the administration has too often failed to acknowledge the efforts of its players, with a notable exception. Ray Baartz, arguably the most skilful home-grown player of any generation, fell victim to a savage karate chop from Uruguayan Luis Garisto in a 'friendly' international played just two months before the 1974 World Cup finals. It was an injury which was to end his career at the age of 27, although as he lay partly paralysed in a bed in North Shore Hospital it was likely that walking rather than playing again was uppermost in his mind. After playing such a key role in helping the Socceroos to the finals, it seemed fate would deny Baartz his moment in the sun. But to the credit of the Australian Soccer Federation, it was agreed his airfare to Germany and accommodation would be paid to ensure he was a member of the World Cup party—a commendable, and welcome, gesture.

Sadly, it remains an isolated one. It is to the chagrin of Warren, for instance, that only in Australia are the officials still generally better known than the players. 'Until that changes, we will never progress,' he said.

It may not have been noticed at the time, but perhaps the most telling statistic of Australia's 1974 success was contained in the teamsheet for the opening match against East Germany. Of the 11 players named in the starting line-up, only two—Col 'Bunny' Curran and John 'Skippy' Warren—were born in Australia, but it proved to be a watershed for the influence of the imported players on domestic playing standards. The pendulum had started to swing. The 1974 team provided the necessary inspiration for a whole generation of local players to work hard, to listen, and to learn. Slowly but surely, the game would become 'Australianised'—not dominated by one ethnic group or another but helped along by an assimilated football culture in which the foreign-sounding names of the future would actually

THE INHERITANCE

be second- and third-generation Australians. And the game would be all the better for it.

By the time the Socceroos stepped back into the breach for the 1977 World Cup qualifiers, much had changed already. Of course there was a new coach, although Jimmy Shoulder did not directly replace Rasic. In fact three coaches had occupied the hot seat in the meantime. Two of them, Eric Worthington and Tony Boggi, had been there on a caretaker basis. Then followed the short-lived but sensational tenure of Englishman Brian Green, who lasted just a year in the post before leaving the country in shame after being convicted of stealing two LPs from a record store. With less than a year to go until the World Cup campaign, the national team was again left without a coach. Applications were called for and 23 were received. Rasic put his hat in the ring, and was heavily favoured, but interstate politics were to play a crucial role. New South Wales, having failed to get either Rasic or Warren past the first ballots, then decided to vote against Victoria's preferred candidate, Alan Vest. Virtually by default, Shoulder, a little-known 29-year-old Englishman, was the successful candidate. Sir Arthur George fumed. 'You got the coach you deserved,' he told the New South Wales delegate as he left the room. Soccer had shot itself in the foot again, and the coach was left to carry the can.

Shoulder did a reasonable job in a trying environment. The likes of Jim Rooney, Wilson, Harry Williams and Abonyi remained from the 1974 side, but Shoulder also gave several promising local players their chance. Youngsters such as John Kosmina, Allan Maher, Gary Byrne, Murray Barnes and Peter Stone all figured regularly during another long and arduous campaign. Having disposed of Oceania rivals Taiwan and New Zealand with ease, the Australians were then pitted against the four Asian group winners—Iran, Kuwait, Hong Kong and South Korea—for the one available place in the 1978 finals in Argentina. It turned out to be too sharp a learning curve for a new-look team under a rookie coach. Apart from two workmanlike victories over the easybeats, Hong Kong, the Socceroos could muster only one win and four losses against the stronger Asian teams. The issue was settled as early as the second qualifier against Iran in Melbourne. Dave Harding missed a penalty and the visitors triumphed 1–0 to exact sweet revenge for their own defeat on Australian soil four years before. It was all downhill for the Socceroos from there, with the only bright spot a gritty win over South Korea in Sydney.

Brazilian coach Carlos Alberto Parreira, then in charge of Kuwait, had few kind words to say about the Socceroos after his team had won 2–1 at the Sydney Sportsground. 'Australia is not a team. It is a joke. The Australians have no imagination, no organisation, no tactical knowledge at all. They let you know in advance every move they make.' It was a harsh assessment, but a prophetic one. When the inevitable eventually became a reality after another loss to Kuwait in Kuwait City, there was much hand-wringing about where it had all gone wrong, and who was responsible. In truth, it was a collective responsibility. Australia had made some progress in important areas—the national league had been formed that year, while the national coaching system established by Worthington was making inroads into improving the education of young players—but there was one ingredient sadly lacking: money. The Asians had lots of it and were prepared to invest. Australia remained impoverished in comparison.

What resources the game did possess would have been best spent in improving things from the ground up. And to the credit of the Australian Soccer Federation, that is exactly what they had planned. As the post-mortems into the 1977 failure got underway in earnest, there was consensus on one key factor—it was time for Australia to seriously nurture and develop its own talent. The players were good enough, as Kosmina and his peers had demonstrated. They just needed the encouragement, the facilities, the coaching, and the opportunity. When German Rudi Gutendorf arrived in 1978 to take over the national team, the will was there and framework was in place. A year later Australia fielded a youth (under-19) team for the first time, and a new era had begun. It was players from this youth system, soon to be complemented by the establishment of a soccer program at the Australian Institute of Sport (AIS) in Canberra, that would provide the backbone of the national team in the years to come. But if Gutendorf, under instruction from his employers, is remembered for getting the youth system off the ground, he was not to last long enough to enjoy the fruits of his labours.

Of all the World Cup campaigns undertaken by the Socceroos, the 1981 effort will go down in history as the least successful. In effect, it never got past first base. The Oceania group hardly loomed as a daunting challenge, or so it was thought. But the World Cup was over as a contest inside the first two games. Arch rivals New Zealand finally got one over their traditional enemy. A 3–3 draw in the opening match in Auckland provided a hint of things to come, with the Socceroos squandering the lead on three occasions. Three weeks later, those misses came back to haunt the team. New Zealand won 2–0 in the return match at the Sydney Cricket Ground, a defeat which ranks as probably the most humiliating in Australia's World Cup history.

Gutendorf, whose eccentric methods had almost caused a mutiny during a

THE INHERITANCE

European tour six months earlier, was sacked in the hours after the match. Australia fulfilled its qualifying obligations against Chinese-Taipei, Fiji and Indonesia by mostly fielding the youth team, then preparing to host the World Youth Championships. Scheinflug, who had been Gutendorf's assistant, took charge. If there was a silver lining to a very black cloud, it was that youngsters such as David Mitchell, Jim Patikas, Alan Davidson and Oscar Crino all got their chance, and were destined to play prominent roles in the next campaign. Indeed if 1981 marked the lowest ebb in Australia's quest for World Cup glory, then 1985 represented a resurrection. Much of it was down to the Arok factor. After waiting patiently for his chance, Arok was finally given the post he deserved midway through 1983.

Scheinflug had elected to follow the Young Socceroos to the World Youth Championships in Mexico, leaving Arok in control of the national team for a prestigious three-match tour by England. This decision cost Scheinflug, the perennial assistant, his one and only chance to take the Socceroos into a World Cup campaign. Arok did so well against the English (two draws and a single-goal defeat) that he was handed the job on a full-time basis. It was no more than he deserved. Unlike so many of his predecessors—and those who would follow—Arok was a devout believer in the cause. The Socceroos represented everything he had always wanted, and he was absolutely determined not to squander his opportunity. His mind, his being, was consumed by his commitment. And although he was obliged to divide his time between the Socceroos and his beloved St George, he combined the two jobs so well that Saints won the national league in 1983, and would figure regularly in the finals in the years to come. But it was the national team which took Arok's passion for Australian soccer to a new plane.

'I would say the team's self-belief, its self-esteem, got lost somewhere between 1974 and when Frank took over,' said Kosmina. 'What he did was re-establish credibility. He gave the players back their pride in the shirt. And what I liked most about him was that he wasn't afraid to pick strong characters. He wanted a team of bastards, and he got it.'

That team turned out to be one of the most respected Australia has ever produced. After two years of planning, Arok took the Socceroos into the 1985 World Cup campaign convinced it would take a very good opponent to deny them a place in the finals. He was right. Australia got to within two games of a place in Mexico 86 only to be thwarted by a Scotland team blessed with world-class talents such as Kenny Dalglish, Graeme Souness, Gordon Strachan and Davie Cooper. If there was some consolation, it was that many Scots still rate that side as their best ever.

It wasn't a bad Australian team, either. Kosmina was at the peak of his powers, a fearless leader and a world-class striker, playing at the sharp end of a team which had a backline of steel (Ratcliffe, Yankos, O'Connor), a midfield blend of strength (Murphy) and skill (Crino and Watson), and a goalkeeper (Greedy) who was never given the credit he deserved. On the fringes of the first XI was a posse of talented, hungry young Australian-born players such as Arnold, Farina, Patikas and Davidson ready to step in and perform at every invitation. It says much about Arok's foresight that in the midst of one World Cup campaign he already had an eye on the next.

In the 1985 preliminaries, Arok had to rely on the hard heads to tackle New Zealand and Israel in an Oceania qualifying group which once again included Asia's political outcasts, Chinese-Taipei. There were some testing moments, never more so than in the second game in Tel Aviv when Greedy was knocked out and helped groggily off the pitch while Arok was banished from the stadium for cursing the Italian referee. With the coach watching most of the match from a vantage point of a wooden crate propped behind a barbed wire fence, the Socceroos showed immense character to win the game 2–1, thanks to two superb strikes from Mitchell and Kosmina. It was the foundation for an epic campaign. The Israelis flew into Melbourne a week later intent on revenge, but only found an Australian team more motivated than it had been in Tel Aviv. Another bad-tempered match saw the teams share a 1–1 draw, with Israel's chances of a victory destroyed by the second half dismissal of their star striker, Eli Ohana. The Israelis were left hoping that New Zealand would do them a favour in the final game of the section in Sydney two weeks later, but the Socceroos were in no mood to relinquish their hard-won advantage. Another classic goal from Kosmina steered the Socceroos to a 2–0 victory—enough to win the Oceania group.

It was not enough to get the team to Mexico, however. Scotland barred the way in a home-and-away series, and few expected the Socceroos to seriously threaten one of Europe's traditional powers. Unfortunately the Australians were also guilty of putting the Scots on a pedestal. But for their timid approach to the first game in Glasgow they may well have pulled off an upset. 'We gave them too much respect,' admitted Kosmina. A 2–0 win at Hampden Park, highlighted by a clever free kick converted by Cooper, left the Socceroos with a mountain to climb in the return leg to be played in Melbourne. Arok had wanted the match, which was scheduled for early December, to be played in the heat and humidity of Darwin or Brisbane, but was overruled by his employers. Instead, on a balmy evening and on a beautifully manicured pitch at Olympic Park, the Scots held on for a scoreless draw to win

T/H/E I/N/H/E/R/I/T/A/N/C/E

their way into the finals. The Socceroos, who had squandered a host of opportunities, could only chafe in frustration. Scotland may have had the tradition and prestige, but nobody in the Australian squad could accept they had a better team.

It was a feeling shared by Arok, who had seen enough to be confident that the future was in good hands. 'We had gone from the British style, where we played the long ball and fought for everything, to being able to play a certain system with players who could hold the ball,' he recalled. 'The imports were going and these beautiful Australian kids were coming through in their place. We had showed the world we could be someone, and I was certain things would start to get better.'

Arok kept his job in a rare show of faith by Soccer Australia, which had briefly considered the claims of his assistant, Eddie Thomson. The two men were total opposites in character and style, but they had proved to be a successful partnership. Eventually, however, something would have to give, for Thomson continued to make little secret of his desire for Arok's job. Things came to a head at the Seoul Olympics of 1988, when Thomson resigned as assistant after the quarterfinal loss to Brazil. It seemed to be strange timing, but Thomson had been promised by at least one high-ranking official that he would get the top job for the 1989 World Cup qualifiers. As it happened, Arok's success in taking the Socceroos through to the final eight of the Olympic Games—by far the highest level the team had ever achieved—made it impossible for him to be sacked. Thomson would have to cool his heels as Arok was given a second shot at World Cup glory.

Sadly for Arok, events conspired against him. No sooner had the triumphant team returned home from the Olympics, than Arok was told by Soccer Australia he would have to open the World Cup campaign two months later—out of season and in the heat of Fiji. The Socceroos lost 1–0 on a bumpy pitch in Nadi, and the poor decision-making by Soccer Australia looked set to cost the team dearly. 'Of course we should never have agreed to such crazy scheduling, but these people didn't seem to care,' said Arok.

The Socceroos recovered to thrash the Fijians 5–1 in the return leg match in Newcastle—a match which featured an all-in brawl—but the campaign was soon to go off the rails once again.

The 1989 World Cup campaign marked the first time the national team had been forced to rely heavily on players based overseas. Four years earlier, the team's only expatriate, Mitchell, had returned home to play in the national league before the qualifiers began. But this time first-choice players such as Farina, Mitchell, Krncevic and Yankos were all contracted and playing for European clubs as the games against New Zealand and Israel approached. With Farina, Yankos, and Krncevic on the park, the Socceroos did well enough to draw with Israel in Tel Aviv. Their respective clubs (FC Brugge, PAOK Salonika and Anderlecht) had been reasonably accommodating, but when their players suddenly asked to travel 20 000 kilometres to play in the remaining World Cup games in mid-season, things started to get difficult. Yankos, the captain, took matters into his own hands and made himself available for the matches against New Zealand in Sydney and Auckland. Farina, Mitchell and Krncevic, however, chose to wait until the final match against Israel. By that stage everything hinged on the result.

Australia had thrashed New Zealand 4–1 in Sydney, but then had gone to Auckland for the return match and surrendered meekly to a defeat which was to have disastrous repercussions. Israel had believed they were out of the frame after drawing at home to the Socceroos, but they had unexpectedly been handed a reprieve. To reach the next and final stage of the campaign (a play-off against Colombia) the Israelis found themselves needing only to draw the return match against Australia at the newly-opened Sydney Football Stadium, built on the site of the old Sportsground. A record crowd of over 43 000 crammed into the stadium, with thousands more turned away. Arok had gambled heavily by selecting Mitchell, Farina and Krncevic in his starting side despite their late arrivals from Europe, and it was a ploy that backfired. A sluggish Socceroo team lacked the fluency and cohesion to force the issue, and when Israel went ahead after a rare mistake from Yankos, the cause was effectively lost. A late equaliser from substitute Paul Trimboli salvaged pride, but little else. Once again, tragically so, Australia was out of the World Cup. It was scant consolation that Israel, too, fell at the final hurdle.

A frustrating record of underachievement stretching back over more than two decades now stood at one success in seven attempts. But if the storyline seemed to have a recurring theme, much had changed since the first World Cup outing to Cambodia in 1965. For the first time, the national team was able to call upon a core of foreign-based professionals—the game had progressed from being an importer to an exporter of talent. Eventually, after a phoney war which lasted a year, Thomson finally got his wish when he was appointed to succeed Arok as national coach in mid-1990. How would he deal with this brave new world? Times were changing rapidly, too rapidly for some. But Thomson believed he could handle the climate of change. Arok was not so sure. The two men would rarely speak to each other again, but they did agree on one thing—the Socceroos badly needed to get to the World Cup finals again. And soon.

Previous page: Mark Bosnich scores from the penalty spot during Australia's 13–0 victory over the Solomon Islands at Parramatta Stadium. CLAYTON/THE SYDNEY MORNING HERALD
Above: Australia's Ned Zelic out jumps Moise Tetuanui of Tahiti at Parramatta Stadium.
CLAYTON/THE SYDNEY MORNING HERALD

Previous page: Craig Foster in action against New Zealand in a World Cup qualifying match. CLAYTON/THE SYDNEY MORNING HERALD
Above: Aurelio Vidmar scores Australia's second goal at New Zealand's North Harbour Stadium in Auckland. CLAYTON/THE SYDNEY MORNING HERALD

CHAPTER 3

THOMMO'S RULE

THE EDDIE THOMSON ERA WAS BEST encapsulated in one commentary published upon his departure: a good beginning, a fair middle, and a poor ending. After promising so much, Thomson delivered much less than had been hoped for. Not necessarily in terms of the World Cup, for the 1993 campaign had its moments—especially in the final stages which produced two of the biggest and most memorable matches the Socceroos have ever played. But it became a real source of frustration to many that a coach blessed with such widespread support at the time of his appointment could squander virtually all of it. And in comparison to those who went before him, Thomson did enjoy a number of significant advantages. First and foremost, the players were right behind him—certainly at the start. Secondly, he had the ear of most sections of the media. Thirdly, he inherited a team left in good shape by Arok and only likely to get better. And last, but certainly not least, he was given substantially more financial, logistical and political support than most of his predecessors.

So what went wrong? Why did a coach blessed with such a keen tactical eye and a rare gift for dressing-room camaraderie end up quitting his post prematurely, leaving a great deal of acrimony in his wake? There was a multitude of reasons, one being the decisions made by Thomson himself. In many ways, the man who arrived in the post in mid-1990 and the man who left it in mid-contract six years later were two different people. Thomson lost his sense of perspective, which had always been regarded as one of his greatest strengths. Because of this, he was to find himself embroiled in perhaps the biggest controversy in the game's history, fighting for his career, his reputation, his future. He was strong enough to still be standing at the end, but the cost was high—both in personal terms, and in terms of his legacy to the Socceroos. It was an episode the game could have, and should have, done without.

The root cause of the controversy was the transfer of Australian players to overseas clubs. And it was Thomson's role in this process that triggered the dramatic sequence of events in 1994 and 1995. If the Thomson era is remembered for one thing, it is for the Stewart Report and subsequent Senate Inquiry. These successive investigations threatened to tear Australian soccer apart, causing many friendships to be shattered as players, coaches, officials and even the media were forced to take sides. Many would argue the game has yet to be put back together again.

The decision to hold formal, public investigations into a raft of allegations concerning the activities of various soccer officials in the overseas transfer market was made belatedly and with great reluctance. But it was a decision Soccer Australia could no longer avoid. Rumours about who was organising the increasingly lucrative trade in Australian players to European clubs, and why, had been circulating within the game as far back as 1990. Thomson's decision to keep close company with European agents such as Israel Maoz, Graham Smith, Frank McKlintock and Ton van Dalen led to whispered questions about the level of his own involvement. In time, some of his biggest critics would be key members of his own national squad.

The rumours began to gather serious momentum before, during and after the Barcelona Olympics of 1992. While Thomson's chief responsibility was to the Socceroos, his job description also meant he was head coach of the Australian under-23 team, the Olyroos. An outstanding crop of emerging talent came together for Barcelona, and during the course of a memorable Olympic campaign the side stamped itself as one of the best Australia had ever produced. The Olyroos went all the way to the semifinals, where they were thumped 6–1 by a superb Polish team in a match that was nowhere near as one-sided as the scoreline suggests. Australia's fourth placing remains arguably the high-water mark for the nation's achievements on the world stage.

Yet instead of returning home to display their talents in the domestic league, the likes of David Seal, Steve Refenes, Ned Zelic, Shaun Murphy, John Filan and Tony Vidmar dispersed to a multitude of European clubs almost as soon as the Olympics were over. It was this 'fire sale' of so many outstanding young players which increased the pressure on Soccer Australia to tackle Thomson on his behaviour.

Chairman John Constantine, who had been aware of the speculation for at least a year, decided it was time to confront his coach.

> 'I pulled him in as soon as he got back from Barcelona and basically said "Eddie, stay as far away as possible from these transfers". I felt he was not doing himself any favours by putting himself in a position where people could make accusations. The perception was that he was too close to the transfers, but his reply was always the same: if players wanted advice, he felt he was the best person to give it to them.
>
> 'I think if Eddie had been a bit smarter, he might have done things differently. But I guess that's easy to say with the benefit of hindsight.'

A code of conduct, nonetheless, was inserted into Thomson's contract and that of his assistant, Scheinflug, shortly after Thomson's discussions with Constantine. This clause expressly forebade either coach from being actively involved in overseas transfers. Incredibly, the contracts were not signed off until three years later—an amazing oversight in view of the prevailing climate of mistrust and suspicion.

In fact, Thomson did little to distance himself from the thorny subject of transfers, resorting instead to publicly defending his stance. He told the *Australian* just a few months after the Barcelona Olympics: 'I admit I helped the players with their contracts, but there is absolutely nothing wrong with that. I felt it was my duty. I had been with some of the lads for two years and I was not going to see them get ripped off.'

However it was an issue that simply refused to disappear. Six months later, the Football Association in England conducted its own investigation into the operations of First Wave Management, a company owned by Smith and McKlintock. Caught in the trap were three Australian players, Bob Catlin, Shaun Murphy and Mark Bosnich, who had all bought out their own contracts to expedite their moves overseas.

The FA found that First Wave had been paid over $600 000 in transfer fees by the purchasing clubs (Notts County and Aston Villa), but that the selling clubs in Australia had received a paltry $43 000 in compensation. Yet because the company was outside the FA's jurisdiction, it could not be sanctioned. And the players themselves had broken no rules. Instead, both Aston Villa and Notts County were fined heavily for paying transfer money directly to an agent.

Catlin may have escaped censure, but he learned his lesson well. The burly goalkeeper, who returned to Australia in 1995, angrily confronted Smith while attending a training camp for the Socceroos at the Papendal complex in Holland.

'Basically, I was annoyed because I had been lied to,' Catlin said. 'I had been led to believe by Smith that he was going to get a spotter's fee, that's all. Then my club (Notts County) told me they had paid him £75 000 for my transfer. The way I saw it, that was money that should have gone to me. Like a lot of boys, I had been too trusting. I was naive.'

The FA inquiry only served to increase the pressure on Soccer Australia to make a more serious attempt to regulate the market at its end. The day after the FA began its inquiry, Soccer Australia chief executive Ian Holmes announced he would open his own internal investigation into all overseas transfers since 1985. Thomson was not mentioned specifically, but he need not have been concerned. Just two days after Holmes's statement, Constantine poured a bucket full of cold water on the proposal. The chairman insisted that new FIFA regulations preventing players from buying out their own contracts—a practice encouraged by agents as a way of increasing their commission—had made any such inquiry redundant. 'It is a dead issue as far as I'm concerned,' he told the *Sydney Morning Herald*. As it happened, however, nothing could have been further from the truth.

As the national youth (under-23) team prepared to host the 1993 World Youth Championships, scouts and agents from around the world descended on the country to assess the next generation of world-class talent, Smith and van Dalen among them. Thomson again kept in close company, and he continued to publicly promote the talent drain, claiming in one article: 'Even if we go professional we can never offer the kids the glamour that comes with playing in Europe or South America. So overseas has got to be a good option.'

In effect, Thomson was making a rod for his own back. By actively encouraging local players to leave the country, he was depriving himself of the use—on a regular basis—of players for his own national team. Yet the obvious pitfalls of this public stance failed to dawn on his employers. Thomson was never censured for his comments. But every time the national coach made his views known in the press, Soccer Australia found it increasingly difficult to deflect attention from the subject.

Half-hearted attempts were made to circumvent the issue. Soccer Australia considered appointing an official players' agent, and Constantine interviewed former Socceroo Eddie Krncevic and Israel Maoz for the role. Another former international, Peter Tredinnick, who had retired to become a partner in a leading Sydney law firm, was also approached. But despite the clear benefits of making an official appointment to handle overseas transfers on a transparent basis—and in so doing dampen down the speculation surrounding Thomson and others—nothing was done. The rumours continued to bubble beneath the surface. They had to rise to the top sooner or later, and they did.

A flurry of media reports in May 1994 brought the issue to mainstream attention for the first time. The magazine *Inside Sport*, the sister newspapers the *Sun Herald* and the *Sydney Morning Herald*, and the ABC current affairs show 'Four Corners', all weighed into the debate. Suddenly the pressure had reached boiling point. The clamour grew for an independent inquiry into the allegations. And when the players' union, the Australian Soccer Players Association (ASPA), also threw its support behind an inquiry, the time for hesitation was over. On 28 May 1994, Soccer Australia's president, Neville Wran, told the ABC's 'Grandstand' program: 'This matter needs to be put to rest one way or another.' Six days later Wran announced that a former New South Wales Supreme Court judge, Donald Stewart, had been appointed to head an independent inquiry. The terms of reference were to (1) inquire into the practices and procedures of the transfer of players from one club to another, (2) investigate practices and procedures relating to the payment of commissions, (3) investigate practices and procedures applied in the selection of players to the national squads and to inquire into any acts of impropriety in such process and (4) to draft a code of conduct.

The day after the inquiry was announced, Thomson told the *Australian*: 'I cannot believe what is going on. How many times do I have to say it? I have done nothing wrong. My conscience is clear.' Stewart, however, was ultimately to disagree. After taking evidence from 60 witnesses in five cities, his report hit the desks of Soccer Australia's headquarters at Rockdale six months later. It was like a time bomb. While seven high-ranking identities were named adversely in his report, it was Stewart's recommendation that Thomson be sacked immediately that caused an uproar. Soccer had made the front page headlines, but for all the wrong reasons.

'When I look back, I believe the mistake we made was having the terms of reference so wide,' said Constantine. 'I still think it could have, and should have, been kept in-house. Nothing positive was achieved at all. It didn't change the ground rules, it didn't clean anything up. Most of the allegations were found to have no substance. It was just an opportunity seized upon by certain people to vent their venom.'

Stewart, who had a long background in royal commissions and was widely respected in legal circles, conceded the flaws in his inquiry when he presented his report to Soccer Australia in early December 1994. He admitted he had had no power to force anybody to present evidence, he had no power to charge anybody, and he was affected by a host of constraining factors. But he believed he had tapped into the mood of the time, he strongly defended his own judgements, and he felt his report possessed enough substance to support his recommendations. Stewart also believed, privately, that the process of investigation could be taken a step further with either a royal commission or a government inquiry which had the benefit of parliamentary privilege.

Stewart had certainly acted with the best intentions. While Soccer Australia was to eventually devote a great deal of time and energy to discrediting the Stewart Report, nobody could question the author's honesty. It was that honesty which gave him the courage to deliver a report which he knew would rock the game, and its administration, to the core. The first report was withdrawn and subsequently amended after both Constantine and Holmes approached Stewart to say they may have given misleading evidence. The evidence in dispute was whether Thomson had a code of conduct in his contract before or after the Barcelona Olympics. It was ultimately proven that this clause was not inserted until after he had returned home. But that was not enough to deter Stewart from repeating his most stunning recommendation in his second and final report. The services of Thomson, he said, should be terminated 'as soon as possible'.

In the eyes of Stewart, the key event had been Thomson's decision to leave the Olyroos' camp at Papendal and travel to Germany to help negotiate the transfer of Ned Zelic from Sydney Olympic to Borussia Dortmund. Stewart found that although there was no evidence that Thomson had received any renumeration for his involvement, his behaviour had nonetheless been 'highly' improper, and warranted dismissal.

Because of the real danger of a stream of expensive defamation litigation, Soccer Australia had a problem with how to make public the report. Clearly, given the community interest surrounding Stewart's inquiry, it could not be kept secret. So it was eventually decided to release with the protection of parliamentary privilege, via a Senate committee established for just such a purpose. That committee, in turn, opted to set up its own inquiry to review the recommendations of the Stewart report.

For six months the game continued to be buffeted by scandal, but Thomson held firm. Soccer Australia, for its part, refused to act on any of the recommendations until after the Senate had completed its own deliberations. But the controversy was to cost Constantine his job. The chairman eventually decided to resign for two reasons. He had been denied the full backing of his board for his handling of the Stewart Report, and his own law practice was being badly affected by the demands on his time from what, after all, was a part-time position. Constantine, undoubtedly, did the honourable thing. For the mood for a revolution was ripe.

Shortly after the Senate got its inquiry underway, the revolution manifested itself. Soccer Australia elected a new chairman. The former boss of the ABC and the New South Wales State Railways, David Hill, was swept into office on a platform of reform. Hill had been hand-picked by Wran, who knew him well from his time as New South Wales premier. The new chairman was known to be a decisive, fearless, audacious leader who rarely walked away from a fight. The feeling was that if anybody could guide soccer out of the wreckage, it was Hill. One of his first acts was to make it clear he felt Thomson had no case to answer.

Hill told the Senate inquiry on 7 April 1995: 'I must say that I think Stewart's recommendations in relation to individuals in virtually every single case exceeded the evidence that he presented—in every single case. I think, in that respect, Stewart's report is a shocker.' Hill then made public his full backing of Thomson. The coach would, in fact, be offered a new contract even before the Senate had completed its findings.

The tide had turned dramatically. A coach who had stood on the brink of losing his job in disgrace was—to all intents and purposes—now in the clear. The Senate was subsequently to agree with Hill that Stewart's recommendation to dismiss Thomson had not been justified. But the inquiry did agree with the judge that Thomson's behaviour in the Zelic case had been inappropriate. Later, when the fuss had died down, the Senate would, in its second report, harshly criticise Soccer Australia for taking no action whatsoever against Thomson.

Ultimately, all bar one of Stewart's recommendations regarding individuals were disregarded by the Senate, which had been dogged throughout its hearings by cheap political point-scoring between members of the Government and Opposition. The public, for its part, became disappointed in the Senate's abject failure to uncover any hard evidence despite the strength of its powers. The committee members pointed to the almost complete lack of cooperation from players as its biggest bugbear. It was one subject on which the senators and Stewart agreed. The truth was that the whole process had essentially been instigated on behalf of the players, but, in the words of Stewart, they had failed 'to stand up and be counted'. Ironically, on one memorable afternoon three players at the heart of some of the most serious allegations—Paul Okon, Steve Corica and Ned Zelic—were training with the

Socceroos at Sydney's Domain while in the building overlooking the park the Senate inquiry was lamenting their absence. The senators could have called them in from the window.

In the end no Socceroo, apart from South Melbourne midfielder Mike Petersen, was brave enough to give evidence to either Stewart or the Senate Inquiry. Thomson kept his job and enjoyed the benefit of a new, upgraded contract. But, quite understandably, he was bitter about the experience and made no secret of his distaste for those he believed had conspired against him.

'Eddie was very disappointed that some of his so-called friendships had disappeared so quickly,' said Constantine. 'But one thing it did do was bring the two of us closer together. The easiest thing in the world for me to have done at that stage would have been to give him the sack. It would have taken so much pressure off my shoulders. But I wasn't prepared to do that. To ruin a man's life and his reputation. For what?'

What, indeed? Yet the sad truth was that Thomson had been badly scarred by the episode, and it contributed heavily to his eventual decision to resign from his post just over 12 months later. Having succeeded, in his own mind, in clearing his name, he felt Australian soccer had nonetheless let him down. In the process of winning the damaging, painful battle of wills, he lost much of his motivation to keep going.

That motivation had been rampant at the time of his appointment six years before. Apart from his huge success as a club coach with Sydney City (three championships in a row) and then Sydney Olympic, Thomson had also been a highly popular assistant under Arok. His input had been invaluable, and his tactical knowledge generally regarded as astute. Scottish-born Joe Watson, who played under Thomson for both Sydney City and the Socceroos, was one of a host of admirers. 'He is the best coach I ever played under in Australia,' said Watson.

It seemed a natural progression, then, that Thomson would get the Socceroo post all to himself once Soccer Australia had decided to dispense with Arok's services.

At the time the vacancy arose, Thomson was employed by Soccer Australia as national director of coaching. But a job which required lengthy hours behind a desk was never going to keep him satisfied for long. Having resigned as Arok's assistant at the Seoul Olympics, Thomson had to bide his time during the 1989 World Cup campaign. Instead Arok used local coaches John Margaritis, Gary Cole and Berti Mariani as his assistants.

THOMMOS RULE

When the inevitable became a reality, and Arok was dumped after failing to get the Socceroos across the line in two attempts at the World Cup, Thomson's name was bound to be on top of the list of contenders. As a player, he had scaled the heights of professional football in his native Scotland with both Hearts and Aberdeen. As a coach, he had amply demonstrated his expertise. The Socceroo post was tailor-made for a man born with outstanding leadership qualities.

Having served his apprenticeship for almost 10 years, Thomson was ready, willing and able when the Socceroo job finally became officially available in April 1990. His chances were helped considerably when Constantine, a long-time admirer of Thomson, ousted Ian Brusasco from the chairman's position. But in the interests of accountability, the board decided it should advertise the post both inside the country and around the world. Fate took a hand. Virtually the last application off the fax machine suddenly threw the position wide open.

Josef Venglos, a native of Slovakia, had coached in Australia before, notably a brief spell in charge of the Socceroos during the 1960s. His career had spiralled upwards since then. At the time of his application, Venglos was coaching a successful Czechoslovakian national team. The team was enjoying a superb run under his command, and had just qualified for the 1990 World Cup finals in Italy. So just before Italia 90 began, Constantine flew to Bratislava to see how serious Venglos was about the position. When word leaked out, there were many who believed he was the ideal man for the job. Through his various FIFA roles he was well connected throughout the world, while he also boasted a background and knowledge of the Australian game. Constantine was also impressed, but returned home to claim negotiations had foundered over money. 'His terms were certainly reasonable, but he wanted twice as much as we were able to afford,' said Constantine. A few weeks later, Venglos disputed this claim. Approached in Bari, just after the Czechs had disposed of Costa Rica in a World Cup second round match, he insisted money had not been discussed in detail at all.

Whatever the case, the field was now clear for Thomson to take charge. Scheinflug—who had never seen eye to eye with Arok—would be returned to the national set-up as his assistant. With international demands now requiring Australia to field teams at four levels (under-17, under-20, under-23, and senior), Constantine believed it was important to restructure the program to have two full-time coaches. Thomson and Scheinflug were duly appointed—the former in charge of the senior and Olympic teams, the latter in charge of the under-17s and under-20s. They assisted each other to ensure consistency, in terms of selection tactics.

'I'm very proud of having been responsible for introducing the system,' said Constantine. 'It was a big reason for our success. In time, people came to us from all over the world to study what we had done.'

Certainly the revamped coaching system got off to a solid start. Fourth placings at both the 1992 Barcelona Olympics and the 1993 World Youth Championships improved the nation's international standing. But the crucial test was the 1993 World Cup campaign. As always, only the Socceroos could provide the true barometer of success.

Three Oceania nations—Tahiti, Solomon Islands and Vanuatu—decided to make their World Cup debuts during this campaign. As expected, the island countries ultimately proved to be no match for the traditional regional heavyweights, Australia and New Zealand. Nevertheless the Socceroos, with Thomson preferring to use only home-based players for the early rounds, were given an enormous fright in their opening fixture in Honiara. On a bumpy pitch and before a capacity crowd which included dozens of people sitting in trees overhanging one end of the ground, only a late goal from substitute Tom McCulloch deprived the Solomon Islands of a courageous draw. After this close shave for the Australians, things improved for the visit to Papeete a week later. The power and pace of Carl Veart and Damien Mori proved too much for the Tahitians, who nonetheless were far from embarrassed by the 3–0 defeat. Two away wins to open a World Cup campaign looked good on paper, but in truth the Socceroos had not played particularly well. Thomson's preoccupation with defence, even against teams as weak as Tahiti and the Solomons, did little to encourage his players.

Things actually got worse for the return match against the Tahitians, played at Brisbane's Perry Park. It had been expected that the Socceroos would be more adventurous with the home ground advantage, but once again they found the going tough in front of goal. It required a thundering drive from Mehmet Durakovic, which looped into the net with the aid of a deflection, to add some substance to a 2–0 scoreline. Mathematically, the result ensured the Socceroos would progress to the Oceania play-off, but this was scant consolation. It was even less consolation for the unfortunate Mike Petersen, who was dismissed in a ridiculous decision by the inexperienced Vanuatuan referee. The match would turn out to be the last of Petersen's distinguished career. A gifted player who was rarely given the recognition he deserved, Petersen was overlooked once his suspension was served, and was never selected again. Later in that campaign, when his ability to hold the ball in pressure situations was sorely needed, his absence probably cost the Socceroos dearly.

T/H/O/M/M/O/S R/U/L/E

With the task of winning the group completed, Thomson released the shackles for the final match against the Solomons. Before a pitiful crowd of just over 2000 in Newcastle, the Socceroos finally discovered their shooting boots to thrash the hapless Solomons 6–1, with Veart scoring for the fourth match in succession. But the players were not about to get carried away. They may have done the dirty work in far-flung locations, but there was no doubt in their minds that Thomson would bring back the big guns from overseas for the play-offs against New Zealand six months later. The question which occupied their thoughts was how many of them would remain?

As it happened, not too many. The home-based players were given another chance to stake a claim during a hastily-arranged trip to Singapore to play two friendly matches against Kuwait in early 1993. But Thomson had always intended to rely on his foreign-based professionals when Australia's World Cup future went on the line against New Zealand. Few disputed his rationale. Four years earlier, Arok had been able to call upon only a handful of expatriates. But the trickle had become a flood. Australian players were leaving the country by the planeload. The consensus was that the national team could only benefit from their experience.

Not surprisingly, when the Socceroos lined up against the All Whites at Auckland's Mt Smart Stadium for the first leg of the Oceania play-off, the team was dominated by the 'foreign legion'. Yet for all their impressive credentials, the 'dream team' produced a rusty, disjointed display. It needed a single goal from Graham Arnold, who turned home a miscued shot from Veart, to end a stubborn All Whites resistance. But nobody was complaining. Bitter experience had taught many of the Socceroos that any win in Auckland was to be prized, and the celebrations went long into the night. Few could see the All Whites being able to come back from the dead.

The last rites, in fact, were administered within ten minutes of the return match in Melbourne. Aurelio Vidmar, stung by his omission from the team in Auckland, scored with a superb header, while Veart also found the net to put the tie beyond reach of a dispirited New Zealand team. A rare goal from Zelic—his first for his country—completed the rout.

After a slow start to the campaign, the feeling was the Socceroos had turned the corner. Certainly the overseas-based players had added a new level of skill, and glamour, to the side. But it was not going to be easy. Australia had to wait three months before the identity of their next opponents, drawn from the North/Central American section, became apparent. And even if that hurdle could be overcome, there was still one substantial obstacle barring their way. A play-off against the fourth-best South American team loomed large towards the end of the year. Given Australia's long history of poor treatment in terms of a World Cup qualifying route, it should have surprised no-one that FIFA would heartlessly produce the most difficult path ever. It was demoralising all the same.

But someone forgot to tell the team that the odds had been stacked against them. When Canada were eventually confirmed as their next opponents, the Socceroos felt they were in with a chance. There was drama before the first game in Edmonton, when goalkeeper Mark Bosnich announced he wouldn't be available for the game. Asked to choose between club and country, Bosnich preferred to remain in England and start the new season with Aston Villa. But Thomson, having granted so much latitude to his overseas players in the past, and given the importance of the occasion, was in no mood to compromise. Paul Okon and Frank Farina were recruited against their will, but Bosnich stood his ground. So Thomson asked Soccer Australia to use FIFA rules and suspend him from playing. Bosnich was duly banned from appearing for Aston Villa while the Socceroos were in Edmonton, and he promptly responded by announcing his retirement—at the tender age of 21—from the national team. It was to prove one of the shortest retirements in history.

In the meantime, the burden fell upon Robert Zabica, the impressive Adelaide City custodian, to stand between the posts at the Commonwealth Stadium. Most critics believed the Socceroos had lost nothing by comparison, for Zabica had proved his mettle time and again at international level. Yet there was to be a twist in the tail. Before the game had even settled into a pattern, Zabica was sent off. He was judged to have brought down Canadian forward Dale Mitchell outside the penalty area. After just 15 minutes, the Socceroos found themselves reduced to 10 men in a critical World Cup qualifier away from home.

Thomson reshuffled his side to bring replacement Mark Schwarzer off the bench. A week earlier Schwarzer had not even been in the squad. He was flown to Edmonton only at the last moment when the Bosnich saga reared its head. Now he found himself making his Socceroo debut in the turmoil that followed Zabica's dismissal. By any definition, this was a meteoric rise for the young Marconi goalkeeper. Thankfully, he proved equal to the task.

Down a man for most of the game, it was perhaps no surprise that the Socceroos eventually succumbed to a neat, well-drilled Canadian side. But a crucial away goal, put into his own net by Canadian midfielder Nick Dasovic, gave the team

THOMMOS RULE

heart as it winged its way back to Sydney. Both Thomson and his players were confident the Socceroos would turn things around in the return leg. The Canadians were a team to be respected under their gentlemanly coach, Bobby Lenarduzzi, but they did not intimidate the Australians. The team was optimistic it would set things right before its own fans at the Sydney Football Stadium.

It turned out to be one of the most exciting, nerve-tingling matches ever played by the national team. On a sunlit spring afternoon, the Socceroos charged out of the blocks and pounded Craig Forrest in the Canadian goal. Chance after chance went begging, with Farina perhaps the biggest culprit. It was only right, therefore, that he should redeem himself with a superb goal from a scissors kick to put Australia in front just before the break. The crowd had begun to wonder whether fate was destined to conspire against them. They roared in relief.

Fate was to play a hand midway through the second half; or perhaps, more correctly, it was the hands of Schwarzer which were to play their part. A speculative shot from midfielder Lyndon Hooper somehow slipped through the goalkeeper's outstretched gloves, and Canada were back on level terms. Not only that, but they were ahead on aggregate. The goal threatened to be enough to put the visitors through to the next stage at Australia's expense.

With the clock ticking down, Thomson decided to play his last card. It was a trump. On came the lethal weapon, veteran David Mitchell, who had been cooling his heels on the bench. In his fourth World Cup campaign, Mitchell immediately sparked the Socceroos into life. His bravery in challenging Randy Samuel created the decisive opening. Durakovic lurched towards the dropping ball, and his looping header found its way into the net. The stadium erupted, for a precious lifeline had been secured. Mitchell and Durakovic embraced each other. Years later, these same two players were to become close friends during a stint together with Malaysian club Selangor. It was a relationship that had been forged in adversity.

Durakovic's classic goal tied the scores at 2–2 on aggregate, forcing the match into extra time. But despite continuing to dominate, the Socceroos could find no way through a tough Canadian defence. It would go down to penalties. Russian roulette. It was here, in the white-heat of World Cup survival, that Schwarzer made his name. Twice he saved from the Canadians, and when Farina thumped his penalty into the roof of the net in the last kick of the game, the Socceroos had won the war of attrition. It was an epic, thrilling, unforgettable afternoon. Australia, willed on by the crowd, had done enough to keep the dream alive. For Thomson, this was a match of immense personal satisfaction. Not only a victory, but a victory achieved in style. In many ways, it was to be the high point of his Socceroo career. Thomson savoured the moment, as he deserved to.

Sadly, but perhaps inevitably, the coach was to revert to character for the next and final stage of the 1993 campaign. Australia's opponents turned out to be the team they had least expected to emerge from the South American section. Argentina, twice World Cup holders and with an international record matched only by superpowers Germany and Brazil, inexplicably found themselves in the unprecedented position of fighting for their own survival. An incredible 5-0 loss to Colombia before their own fans in Buenos Aires had pushed the demoralised Argentines through the trapdoor, where the Socceroos were waiting. But help was on the way. Diego Armando Maradona, unquestionably one of the greatest players the game has ever produced, answered the call of his country. Maradona earmarked the play-offs against Australia as the perfect stage for his international comeback after he had served a 15-month ban for a positive drug test.

History will record that these play-offs were the highest-profile matches ever played by our national team. The long-awaited return of Maradona caught the attention of the world, and the stadiums in Sydney and Buenos Aires were packed to the rafters. The games were also televised live throughout the globe.

Inexplicably, Thomson had agreed to play the first leg at home. He defended his decision by saying Australia would have lost the argument anyway, but in truth it was an indefensible position. No other coach in the world would have been happy to have his World Cup fate decided in such a way. Conventional wisdom remains that you get the hard part out of the way and leave yourself with the benefit of home advantage when the tie is to be decided. Yet Thomson claimed he felt comfortable with the prospect of having to chase a second leg result in the cauldron that is the Estadio Monumental in Buenos Aires. The Argentines were, not surprisingly, delighted to humour him.

If it was bad enough that Australia had surrendered the psychological advantage, it was even worse that Thomson went on to surrender the tactical high ground as well. After using Mitchell, a striker, in his training games during the week, the coach decided at the last moment to sacrifice his most experienced forward and bring skipper Paul Wade back into the side instead. Wade, by this stage plagued by ankle problems, was handed the job of marking Maradona. Mitchell was left to fume on the bench. Despite playing at home with their World Cup future at stake, the Socceroos went into the match with just two designated attackers. Once again, Thomson had played right into Argentina's hands.

T/H/O/M/M/O/S R/U/L/E

True enough, the Socceroos were able to create moments of anxiety, the best of them fashioned by Arnold and Slater, but Argentina always looked capable of absorbing the pressure. And when Maradona snatched the ball off Milan Ivanovic and sent a low, flat cross into the middle, trouble loomed. The headlines later credited the goal to Maradona's influence, but in truth his contribution would hardly have been noticed if he had been just another player. It needed a superb header by Abel Balbo, which deceived goalkeeper Bosnich and curled inside the post, to convert the half-chance. The goal looked to have all but extinguished Australia's hopes, but an equaliser arrived when Aurelio Vidmar cleverly turned home a cross from his brother Tony after Zelic had opened up the play. Sadly, but predictably, the second half petered out. The score remained 1–1 at the final whistle. Thomson's cagey strategy had backfired. Now the Socceroos would need at least a score draw in Buenos Aires, where the vociferous backing of the *Ultras* was generally worth at least a goal to their opponents. It was a mountain to climb.

Mitchell was not going up the slope. Straight after the game in Sydney, he stormed out of camp and took a flight home to his parents' house in Adelaide. Not only had he been overlooked at a time when his talents were needed most, but he had only been introduced off the bench when it was all too late. By that stage Mitchell was already stewing over a heated argument he'd had with Thomson in the tunnel just before kick-off. He decided he had had enough. After four World Cup campaigns and 29 caps, Mitchell announced his retirement the following day in a tearful interview with the press. His relationship with Thomson, which went back to their days together with Sydney City in the early 1980s, would never be the same again.

For the Socceroos who did travel to South America, events went according to script. Again the players held the forlorn hope that Thomson would allow them more freedom to attack. Again the coach preferred to err on the side of caution— and this with nothing to lose and everything to gain.

As it was, only a bizarre goal denied the Socceroos the consolation of a respectable scoreless draw. A misdirected cross from Gabriel Batistuta spun off the shin of Alex Tobin, looped into the air and was carried back inside the post by the swirling wind. FIFA later accredited the goal to Batistuta, but even he could hardly claim intent. There were chances at the other end, most of them involving the substitute Veart, but this was never destined to be Australia's night.

As the final whistle was blown by the Danish referee, the Australian players slumped to the confetti-strewn ground. The Argentines, with Maradona leading the cheer squad, went on a lap of honour. There was dignity in defeat, certainly, and the home fans—not known for their sportsmanship—roundly applauded the Socceroos. But again, near enough was not good enough. Later that night, as they drowned their sorrows at various nightclubs, the players pondered what might have been. They had wanted their coach to encourage them to put pressure on their opponents. They genuinely believed that Argentina were not the better side. They were right. But it was Argentina, not Australia, who would be going to the 1994 World Cup finals in the US. One person was especially pleased. In the wee hours at the trendy Trumps nightclub, Maradona paid for the Australian players' drinks.

For Thomson, the play-offs marked the beginning of the end. When a coach loses the faith of his key players, his departure becomes a matter of time. If other events were to provide the trigger for his downfall, it was his failure to recognise just what a good team he had at his disposal which started the rot. The chance to make history had slipped through Thomson's fingers. Not too many coaches are lucky enough to get a second chance.

CHAPTER 4

THE TALENT DRAIN

Looking back, there are many who would say Thomson deserved a reprieve. His supporters still insist that Australia's inability to get past Argentina at the last hurdle before the 1994 World Cup could hardly be defined as a failure at all. There was no doubt, certainly, that the Argentines were the best team the Socceroos had ever faced at World Cup level. And given the subsequent changes to the qualifying system, no Australian team will have to meet such a formidable opponent again. But if Thomson had a strong case to argue that he and his players had performed miracles in daunting circumstances, the near-miss of 1993 must be regarded as a huge disappointment nonetheless. Sure, Argentina boasted a world-class side—a midfield of Redondo, Simeone and Maradona playing behind a forward line of Balbo and Batistuta was an impressive array of talent by any measure. Yet there was another side to the equation. Argentina may have been good, but the Socceroos weren't bad either. And the feeling was that Thomson had never fully appreciated how good his own team was. Which is why the 1993 campaign will be remembered as the one that got away. Even if it was a close thing in the end.

So how could it be that a developing nation like Australia was able to give a first world football power like Argentina such a fright? Thomson knew the answer as well as anyone. The reason the Socceroos suffered little in comparison to their illustrious opponents was because the players had a good idea of what to expect. The likes of Zelic, Bosnich, Slater, Farina, Arnold, Aurelio Vidmar and Okon were all playing with good clubs in good European leagues. The 1993 Socceroos were the first national team to go into a World Cup campaign with more players drawn from outside the country than within. They were the living, breathing, kicking, manifestation of the talent drain. They reflected a changing era—an era in which Australia was rapidly making the transition from an importer to an exporter of talent. As a soccer nation, we had finally grown up.

Generally speaking, the 1980s will be remembered as the decade in which the nation as a whole opened its doors to the world—culturally, politically and economically. The central plank of federal government policy in almost every portfolio was to bring the barriers down, to expose every facet of Australian life to outside influence. Sport was no exception. But of all the sports, soccer was to bear the brunt of this process of globalisation. No other sport had more international appeal. No other sport reflected the country's multicultural identity so obviously. No other sport was better positioned to embrace the new era of free trade. Other sports, notably basketball, would come to feel the same effects, but in the 1980s it was Australian soccer that led the way.

Before the exodus of Australian talent became a phenomenon in its own right, a sprinkling of Australian players had made a fist of playing abroad. It had been more by accident than design, though. Post–World War II, for instance, several Australians remained behind after hostilities had ceased, to play football in England. One of the more successful was Ken Grieves, a handy cricketer who was arguably an even better goalkeeper. Grieves made 147 appearances for a variety of English clubs, among them Bury, Bolton Wanderers and Stockport County, before returning home in 1955. But if Grieves made an impact, it was countryman Joe Marston who truly blazed a trail in the mother country for Australian players. Right up until the late 1970s, Marston was regarded as Australian soccer's most successful export. He played in the 1954 FA Cup final, finishing on the losing side as Preston North End succumbed 3–2 to West Bromwich Albion. Marston played 185 games for Preston before returning to Australia, where he was immediately installed as captain of the national side. In all, Marston played in 35 tests for Australia—a record for any player in the years before soccer's federation (1963). For a long time, however, his exploits weren't given the recognition they deserved. It was not until the early 1990s that Soccer Australia, under pressure to start appreciating its traditions, paid suitable homage by calling the grand final man-of-the-match award the Marston Medal.

A decade after Marston had departed the English scene, two other Australians, John Roberts and Max Tolson, kept the flag flying with mixed success. A few years

T/H/E T/A/L/E/N/T D/R/A/I/N

later Socceroo striker Adrian Alston was recruited by Luton Town during the 1974 World Cup finals and spent three seasons in England (including a spell with Cardiff City) before returning to Wollongong. The only other Australian to make any sort of impression overseas during the mid-1970s was Rene Colusso, a former Marconi junior who spent almost a decade as a professional in Italy's lower divisions.

It was not until Craig Johnston, an all-action midfielder from the shores of Lake Macquarie near Newcastle, arrived in England towards the end of the 1970s that an Australian player made a genuine impact on the international stage. Johnston wrote away, was offered a trial at Middlesbrough, and after enduring the taunts of his young English rivals succeeded in having the last laugh when, on 15 October 1976, he was signed on as an apprentice at Ayresome Park. For the next 12 years Johnston became the icon of Australian soccer, boosting his domestic profile through a highly popular beer commercial. But Johnston, sadly, never played for his country.

In his excellent biography, *Walk Alone*, he would later blame his self-imposed exile on administrative mismanagement. Others, including several key members of the Socceroo team during that era, shared a different view. They believed Johnston had simply never wanted to play for Australia, that he was loathe to interrupt his thriving English club career. Johnston gave credence to this theory when, just as he was embarking on the most successful stage of his career with Liverpool, he produced the infamous quote he would later live to regret. 'Playing soccer for Australia is like surfing for England,' he told interviewer George Negus on '60 Minutes'. It was somewhat ironic, then, that two decades later these same men would plot to revitalise the Socceroos' fortunes in the post-Thomson era. Negus and Johnston played an influential role in the recruitment of Venables, and shared similar visions about the future direction of the game.

Johnston's motivation for getting involved stemmed back to his decision not to play for Australia—a decision that has resulted in a generally hostile reaction whenever he has returned home to visit his family and friends. Johnston's input into the recruitment of Venables, although suspected, was never really confirmed. For a person accustomed to the glare of publicity, his behind-the-scenes role came as a surprise to many. But he had his reasons.

'It goes back to why I didn't play for Australia, why I had no faith, trust or respect for the people running the game at the time,' he said. 'I believed then, and I believe now, they were running the game for the wrong reasons. But because of what happened, I've always had a stigma attached. People look at me and say "you're the bloke who didn't play for the Socceroos". Well I've always wanted to give something back. I couldn't do it as a player, but now I've helped in my own way, and I'm proud of that.'

Johnston the player also had an influence on the international perception of Australian soccer before his premature retirement in 1988. He may never have worn the green and gold, but he flew the flag all the same. Others did, too. John Kosmina (Arsenal) and Alan Davidson (Nottingham Forest) had brief spells abroad, while David Mitchell and Eddie Krncevic were good enough and determined enough to stay. Unlike Johnston, all four played for the national team. But they did have something in common with the Liverpool midfielder: they were the last of the do-it-yourself generation. Going right back to the late 1940s, when Grieves was playing in goal for Bolton, Australian players had to virtually force themselves upon overseas clubs. They were not sought out, they just appeared. But by the time Johnston was winding down his career at Anfield, things were changing dramatically. The talent drain, as we know it, was about to begin.

Several important factors converged to create a climate in which European clubs began to look at Australian players in a new, more positive light. Perhaps most significantly, transfer fees within Europe were going through the roof. The clubs, particularly those that worked at the lower end of the market, were compelled to look for new sources of talent. Australian players were plentiful and cheap, but they were also good. And this was the real attraction: quality players available at a bargain basement price.

The formation of Australia's first youth team in 1979 and the establishment of a soccer academy at the Australian Institute of Sport two years later gave the country a world-class development system. Australia had always had the quantity, but now the quality was coming through via good coaching, good facilities and regular international competition. The fact that the likes of Johnston, Krncevic and Mitchell were not only surviving but flourishing in European competition alerted the clubs and their talent scouts to the steady improvement in the standard of Australian players. The exploits of the Socceroos during the mid-1980s under coach Frank Arok provided further proof. In 1988, the national team upset defending world champions Argentina 4–1 in the Bicentennial Gold Cup. A few months later the Socceroos defeated Yugoslavia in the opening round of the Seoul Olympics, and went on to make the quarter-finals. Throw in the achievements of the 1985 team which ran Scotland close in a World Cup play-off, and Australia's standing in world football was clearly on the rise. Given the inflationary spiral of the European transfer market, it was inevitable that overseas clubs would begin to mine the rich seam of

THE TALENT DRAIN

talent available on the other side the world. With many of these players having family ties in the Old World, the recruiting process was made even easier.

If any single player was responsible for breaking down the barriers once and for good, it was Eddie Krncevic. Almost to a man, previous expatriates had made their way to Great Britain, in particular England. But Krncevic, a lean, lively striker from Marconi-Fairfield, had the courage and the foresight to take a different direction. Given his Croatian heritage, his initial destination of Dinamo Zagreb was no surprise. But his ultimate success on the continent opened up the market for Australians, and led to the trickle of departures turning into a flood.

'I was the first Australian to really make a go of it on the continent,' said Krncevic. 'When I went there was no system, no agents, no real path to follow. But by the time I left there was a whole structure in place to make it easy for young Australian boys to go to Europe. I opened the door for them, and I get a lot of pride out of that.'

Krncevic was approached by Dinamo officials immediately after the Socceroos had lost 4–0 to their side during a European tour under Rudi Gutendorf in 1981. 'I remember the ground was covered in snow, and I didn't think I had a particularly good game,' Krncevic recalled. 'But they came up to me straight after the match and wanted me to sign there and then. I had to go back to Marconi and wait until the end of the season. But it proved to be a good move for me. I was in Zagreb for three years and I couldn't do a thing wrong.'

Yet if Krncevic was welcomed with open arms in Croatia, he was to discover that club football in Europe had a darker, harsher side when he moved to Germany to join MV Duisburg. It was a disastrous choice, something Krncevic still describes as 'the worst six months of my life'.

'They didn't like outsiders, they didn't want to know me,' he said. 'I wasn't invited out by anyone, not even for a coffee, in the whole time I was there. I honestly believe the people were racist. My wife was about to give birth to our second child and I was at the point where I was very close to packing it all in and going home. The impression I got was that the coaches, the players and the fans wondered what the hell an Australian player was doing there.'

Krncevic hung on, leaving Duisburg and moving to Belgium where the culture, the hospitality and the football itself was much more to his liking. Firstly with modest Cercle Brugge, and then with the country's biggest club, Anderlecht, he established himself as one of the Belgian league's most prolific strikers. He won a championship with Anderlecht and became the first Australian to finish as top goalscorer in a European first division competition. It was no coincidence that in the years that followed a host of his fellow countrymen would choose Belgium, or neighbouring Holland, as their first port of call. In the low countries, Krncevic became an inspiration, a father-figure and a spokesman for Australian players destined for the continent. 'I was happy to help any of the boys who came over, because I didn't want them stooged in things like contract negotiations by unscrupulous agents,' he said. 'It's a big learning curve, even now. But things have got a lot easier, and I played a part in that. I'm proud of the fact that guys like Farina, Okon and Aurelio Vidmar were able to keep the torch going.'

Before and after the Seoul Olympics of 1988, Farina and Socceroo teammates Robbie Slater and Vlado Bozinoski arrived in Belgium, to be followed soon after by the likes of Vidmar, Arnold and van Egmond, who all joined Dutch clubs. The next wave included youth internationals Paul Okon and Lorenz Kindtner, and then Tony Vidmar, Dominic Longo and Milan Blagojevic arrived fresh from the 1992 Barcelona Olympic side. In 1982, only four Australians had been contracted to European clubs. A decade later, that number had grown to almost 40. Some of these transfers, particularly those involving Belgian-based agent Israel Maoz, were later to figure prominently in the Stewart Report and Senate Inquiry. The trade in Australian players had, virtually overnight, become big business. Soccer Australia was caught by surprise, and struggled to regulate a burgeoning industry. Australian clubs were often being ripped off, as were the players themselves.

But if the talent drain has created enormous controversy and damaged the quality of the domestic national league in the process, there are many who believe it has had an up-side. The transfer money has certainly been welcomed by the clubs, while a career path has been created for young Australian players. Multi-talented athletes such as cricketer Steve Waugh, AFL player Glenn Jakovich and dual rugby international Michael O'Connor are all examples of promising soccer players who chose other sports because of the money on offer. Now the tide looks to have turned. Socceroo Stan Lazaridis, who played state cricket for Western Australia at youth level, is but one example of a player who has come to recognise that in the 1990s soccer can offer an exciting and rewarding future. For that, he can thank the pioneers who came before him.

Yet it is not at individual level that the impact of the overseas exodus has been most keenly felt. Rather it is the collective example provided by the game's flagship, the Socceroos. For the 1985 World Cup campaign, not a single player was playing his club football outside the country. Four years later, Arok was able to call upon

THE TALENT DRAIN

four expatriates. And when the 1993 team came so near and yet so far against Argentina, Thomson had the luxury of being able to name three teams of foreign-based players if he so desired. By that stage, the concept of having one set of training camps in Australia and another in Europe had gone from imagination to reality. Throughout the early 1990s the various national teams, from under-17 to senior level, made use of the excellent facilities of the Dutch Football Association headquarters at Papendal, near Arnhem. The practice has continued, although the venue has changed since Venables took charge.

If there was one factor that convinced Venables that the idea of taking the Socceroos to the World Cup was not as fanciful as it might have seemed to some of his associates, this was it. There had been a revolution. The game he knew as a touring player with Chelsea in the mid-1960s and the game he would inherit as national coach had changed beyond recognition. At the time of his appointment, there were just over 90 Australians playing professionally outside the country. They were spread between 16 countries from every continent bar Africa. And some of them were playing at the very highest level and not looking out of place. Venables was pleasantly surprised, and impressed.

Seven Australians have tasted action in the Premier League. In Scotland, Tony Vidmar and Craig Moore are regulars with Rangers FC, the league's biggest club. In Italy, Okon is regarded as a prime asset by Lazio. In Germany, striker Paul Agostino has made an impression with 1860 Munich. In France and Spain, Ned Zelic and Aurelio Vidmar were employed by major clubs but were denied regular appearances, not because of their ability but because of internal politics. In Croatia, Mark Viduka and Josip Skoko have been linked to multimillion dollar bids from clubs in Western Europe. And so it goes on. It is for this reason that the expectations of the national team have grown substantially. Australian fans no longer have to study the visiting team to find the stars—nowadays they are more likely to be found wearing the green and gold.

When Venables sized up the opportunity presented to him by David Hill, these were the players who grabbed his attention. These were the players who excited him. These were the players he could see taking Australia to the World Cup. It was why he signed on the dotted line. He was looking forward to getting started.

CHAPTER 5
THE ARRIVAL

AT LONG LAST, HERE HE WAS. THE MESSIAH. The arrival of Terry Venables into Sydney Airport, on the evening of 3 January 1997, created quite a stir. He emerged through Customs wearing an open-necked shirt and blazer, his greying hair stroked back with a wet brush. There was a puffy complexion to a face which had spent the previous 26 hours staring out of an aircraft window, even if the view was from the luxury of a first class seat. Venables' first steps on Australian soil for three decades were scrutinised closely by the bright lights of the television cameras. The flash bulbs popped in unison. Microphones were thrust eagerly towards a mouth which creased into a generous smile. There was a joke, a laugh. Venables, flanked by his wife Yvette, was in his element. Manoeuvred into a briefing room, he was soon ready to face his inquisitors. And as he had done so many times in his career, he played the media off a break, saying something, but saying nothing at all. Generalising. Nothing specific. Nothing that might come back to haunt him. Is there any better exponent of the 30-second grab? And before it seemed to have even got going, it was over. Venables was shepherded out of the room by his minder, Steve Speziale, and into the night.

Officially, Speziale was public relations officer for Soccer Australia unofficially, he was to be at Venables' beck and call for the next five weeks. Duties performed, the new coach and his wife were driven to their accommodation, the Rockwall Apartments in Potts Point. A bottle of Australian chardonnay was waiting in the fridge, alongside a cheese platter. Venables' favourite cigars, Monte Cristos 'ones'

THE ARRIVAL

and 'threes', had been placed on the sideboard. From his balcony on the 16th floor, he sat back, drew heavily on the smoke, and surveyed the twinkling panorama of the city skyline, Harbour Bridge and Opera House. The guv'nor had arrived. The Great Socceroo Adventure was underway.

There were still 15 days before it was down to business—the opening match of the four nations tournament against New Zealand. There were still eight days before Venables would meet his squad of home-based players in Melbourne. In the meantime, there were two priorities—to do more homework on his new team, and to break down the barriers, to press the flesh.

Venables was well aware that his appointment had caused a high level of resentment within the local soccer fraternity. He was mindful that some noses had been pushed out of joint. It wasn't his style to go looking for justification. It wasn't his manner to seek out his detractors. But he did agree to go to the coalface. He did agree to put himself about. If people came up to complain, well, he was ready to stand his ground. Few can work a crowded room better than Venables. Few can disarm their most strident critics so effectively, and so effortlessly. On a personal level, the punters soon warmed to his barrow-boy charm. The new Australian coach was a hard man to dislike.

After his first night's sleep in Australia, Venables was out and about on the hustings the following night. The venue was Marconi Stadium, Bossley Park. The purpose was to watch the national league match between Marconi-Fairfield and the visitors from Perth Glory. This was the true soccer constituency. Here in the stands were plenty of doubters who needed convincing. And on the park, the players would certainly appreciate the presence of the new national coach. There remained a feeling of unease among domestic players that they were destined to be disadvantaged by Venables' decision to continue living in London. By turning up at Bossley Park he was showing, right from the outset, that he was sensitive to their concerns. It may have been a flag-waving exercise, but it was an important duty to perform all the same.

Over the first week, the itinerary read thus: game one, Marconi Stadium; game two, Belmore Sportsground, Sydney Olympic versus West Adelaide; game three, Birmingham Gardens, Newcastle Breakers versus Adelaide City; game four, Bruce Stadium, Canberra Cosmos versus Melbourne Knights. And finally, on the night before he had to turn his attention to the international stage, Venables was guest of honour in the Ray Price Lounge at Parramatta Stadium, watching Sydney United humble the visiting Brisbane Strikers. Five games, ten teams, in three cities over eight days—a crash course in Australian soccer, national-league-style. And some players did manage to catch his expert eye: Hamilton Thorp, a relative unknown for West Adelaide who, six months later, would become the first Australian player to join Portsmouth; Troy Halpin, a clever playmaker for Newcastle who, five months later, earned a surprise call-up for the Superstars series where he was offered words of encouragement; Andrew Marth, formidable as ever for the Melbourne Knights but by his own choice unavailable for the national team. Big 'Stabber' impressed Venables all the same.

Indeed there was a lot Venables found to like about Australian players during that first week. 'He was definitely taken by their natural style and fitness,' said Speziale. Partly, those impressions were gained from his seat in the grandstand. But he also studied hard, spending hours in either his apartment or in the Paddington offices of Soccer Australia poring over videos of Socceroo games. 'Right from the start, Terry made it clear he was here to work,' said Speziale.

Between games, the chance presented itself to visit the player factory which had produced so much of Australia's finest talent. The Australian Institute of Sport is nestled among the rolling hills of the Canberra suburb of Bruce. Venables arrived in the early afternoon and met with the AIS head coach, Steve O'Connor, and AIS director John Boultbee in the soccer office upstairs from the gymnasium. He was taken on a tour of the facilities, including the neatly manicured pitches and the sports science laboratories. England may be the birthplace of the modern game, but its development system is anything but contemporary. The English centre of excellence, Lilleshall, certainly suffered in comparison to the AIS, as Venables conceded.

'I got the impression that he was very impressed,' said O'Connor. 'He was aware of some of the players who had gone through the system, and he seemed very interested in what we had to offer. We gave him a booklet on how we structured our program to take home.'

Venables left the AIS to go next-door to the Bruce Stadium, where Canberra Cosmos were taking on the visiting Melbourne Knights. He was particularly interested in the performance of a recent AIS graduate, Josip Simunic, who a few months earlier had announced his controversial decision to turn his back on Australia in order to declare his allegiance to the country of his parents' birth, Croatia. Simunic had made the decision largely in frustration at being overlooked for the Australian under-23 team for the Atlanta Olympics. He later said publicly that if Venables were to choose him for the senior team, he might be encouraged to change his

THE ARRIVAL

mind. Venables knew of the situation, and was keen to see what he might be missing out on. 'Unfortunately Josip was just coming back from injury and didn't put in one of his better games,' said O'Connor. Simunic never made it into Venables' plans. In truth, Venables already had an embarrassment of riches at his disposal. The task was to mould the putty into shape.

It had been decided that the first opportunity would be given to the local players. The timing of the four nations tournament meant most of Australia's expatriates would be busy with club commitments. Most, but not all. Arnold, Mori and the Vidmar brothers were all visiting home at the time, and were all keen to play. But after discussing the situation with Blanco, Venables decided on the politically-correct course—the domestic candidates would be given first go. For the likes of Alex Tobin, this was vindication. Upon Venables' appointment, the veteran of three World Cup campaigns had said: 'I just don't think anyone should have to apologise for playing here in Australia.' As it turned out, no apologies were necessary.

It was when a sponsor for the January tournament, Optus World, was announced in early December that Venables first made public his intentions. 'I don't want to create an us-versus-them situation, but I think it's only fair the local players get this opportunity,' he declared via satellite from London. Two weeks later he honoured his pledge. The squad of 22 players to play in the four nations tournament would be drawn exclusively from the national league. It was also a squad based largely on the pool of players favoured by his predecessor, Eddie Thomson, although it did contain three uncapped players (Mark Babic, David Zdrilic and Sean Babic) as well as a host of fresh talent on the stand-by list.

After much soul-searching and great anticipation, the squad assembled in Melbourne at the beginning of the third week in January to see and hear exactly what the Brave New World would entail. And to the relief, and delight, of the players, the man himself was not patronising or vain. Venables made it clear he did not want reverence, only respect. It was the enduring trademark of his career—Venables had always been regarded as the quintessential player's coach. It did not matter if it was a group of part-timers in Australia or a collection of superstars at FC Barcelona. The way Venables saw it, take away the size of the pay packet and most players were essentially the same.

This was the message he conveyed to the home-based Socceroos at their opening training session under their new coach, held at the Veneto Club in Bulleen. On a picturesque ground surrounded by bocce courts and gum trees, Venables stood before his charges and delivered his homily. Pictures show the coach, arms in the air, addressing the players seated in a semicircle around him. It looks to be a schoolmasterly pose, but looks can be deceptive. Venables wanted an inclusive relationship from the start.

Craig Foster, reflecting the general consensus, was generous in his praise. 'I learnt more in two hours in that first session than I'd learnt since I left the AIS at the age of 15,' he said. Clearly, Venables—well prepped by Blanco—was keen to get things off on the right track.

And as Venables prepared to take his first bow, the level of interest grew dramatically. Up to 12 countries decided to take television coverage of the match against New Zealand, while a contingent of 30 international journalists—most of them English—received accreditation for the game. 'Where I might be used to getting 20 calls a day, suddenly I was getting between 70 and 80,' said Speziale. 'It was all down to Terry. The interest, at every level, just went through the roof.'

At the Crown Casino three days before the game, Venables was unveiled to the mainstream media and got the chance to renew an old friendship with Keith Pritchett, the New Zealand coach. Pritchett had been a young hopeful in the reserve team at Queens Park Rangers when Venables was captaining the first XI in the mid-1970s. Twenty years may have elapsed, but the bond remained strong. Indeed the conference began to resemble a reunion, with Norwegian coach Egil Olsen also seated on the rostrum. Olsen had successfully plotted the downfall of England on many occasions in recent years—not least when a painful defeat in Oslo all but eliminated the English from the 1994 World Cup. Olsen expressed no surprise at travelling across the world and finding his old adversary in a new guise. 'If you are a professional coach, then you must be prepared for new adventures,' Olsen said.

Being adventurous was ingrained in Venables' nature, and not only off the pitch. During a relaxed buildup to his opening game in charge—the players were excused from training for a day to watch the Australian Open tennis—one observation emerged clearly above all else. Venables wanted his new team to attack.

It was a breath of fresh air. The players, finally unburdened of the defensive straitjacket imposed by the dour tactics of Eddie Thomson, relished the challenge. In the lead-up to the New Zealand match, the training was based on getting the ball forward. Not recklessly—Venables spent plenty of time working with the three-man defensive unit. But his foundation was to get forward movement, both on and off the ball. The buzz among the players back at the hotel was that, at last, they had a coach who believed in them. Finally they were to be encouraged to test the limits of their ability. Finally they were to play in an Australian team which would

THE A/R/R/I/V/AL

take the game to their opponents. Finally a draw would no longer be regarded as a satisfactory result. Finally the Socceroos were to become a team geared to winning. And preferably winning with panache, with style. What a relief!

Raul Blanco, the assistant, deserved credit for the change. Blanco had long favoured players with skill, with vision, with flair. He had also chafed, privately, at the way the national team had too often played within itself. Having worked so long with the national junior teams, Blanco was a strong believer in the quality of Australian talent. It just needed to be encouraged, that was all. Over intensive video sessions and persuasive argument, he had helped Venables to come to the conclusion that the Socceroos did, indeed, have the players to take the game to the opposition. Venables also appreciated just how desperate the public and the players were to see the Socceroos emerge from their shell. So the new coach agreed that attack would be the best form of defence. It was the smartest move he could ever have made.

Which is not to say such a drastic change in approach was going to work overnight. With barely a week together with his team, Venables expected teething problems against New Zealand. And he got them. But he got off to an encouraging start all the same.

The curtain went up on the Venables reign at modest Lakeside Stadium, home of South Melbourne. Seven months earlier he had sat in the dugout at Wembley Stadium as England, watched by 90 000 fans, went on to lose a dramatic European Championship semifinal against their nemesis, Germany. Now Venables was poised to return to the international arena, but that was where the similarity ended. Lakeside's capacity is just 12 000 and it was full to the brim for the early match between South Korea and Norway. But by the time Venables took his team down the tunnel, the Korean fans were already streaming to the exits. There were noticeable gaps in the terraces when the main game kicked off—yet again a sure sign that, Venables or not, the Socceroos continued to struggle for mainstream acceptance.

Ultimately, they were also forced to struggle for a face-saving 1–0 win. By playing three attacking players—Trimboli, Trajanovski and Zdrilic—the right intent was there. And things began brightly enough, with the speed and mobility of the Australians constantly tormenting the ponderous All Whites defence. Chances came thick and fast, but New Zealand goalkeeper Jason Batty was proving to be a resolute last line of defence. Midway through the first half, Batty was finally beaten, and the Venables influence was evident. A quick throw from goalkeeper Kalac was collected by Trajanovski on the right, and his through ball found the rampaging

Bingley, who rounded Batty and slipped the ball into the net. Fittingly, the three best Australian players on the night were involved. Fittingly, it was the surging run through the middle from Bingley—nominally a wing-back—which created the opening. A player who had barely crossed the halfway line under Thomson found himself in unchartered territory. And it worked.

Australia tried to force home their advantage, but in the second half New Zealand regrouped. Kalac saved the Socceroos on several occasions as All Whites striker Darren McClennan hustled his way through an uncertain defence. Five changes—two of them forced—had interrupted the Socceroo game-plan. But the home side hung on, and at the final whistle Venables embraced his assistant, Blanco. The new era was off to a winning start.

'It was a lot like we thought, a highly competitive game—a lot like a local derby,' said Venables. 'New Zealand weren't there for us to run over. I thought in the first half we did very well, but then we dropped off and gave them space. There's no doubt the players know they can do a lot better.'

But a black cloud was looming on the horizon as the squad flew from Melbourne to Brisbane, where the second match of the series, against the lively Koreans, was due to be played. Money was on the minds of the players. They wanted more.

A dispute which pre-dated Venables had come to a head. The players' union, the Australian Soccer Players Association, maintained it had reached an agreement with Soccer Australia following the Oceania Nations Cup final three months earlier. The thrust of the claim, which included revenue-sharing and bonuses for the World Cup campaign, was based on protecting the interests of the local players. By beating Tahiti to win the Oceania Cup, the Socceroos had qualified for the lucrative Confederations Cup tournament. But the players and their union knew that by the time the tournament would be staged in Saudi Arabia 12 months later, it would be overseas-based players, and not the locals, who would be involved. The intent was to ensure an even distribution of whatever money was to be generated over the course of the World Cup qualifiers and the Confederations Cup (by most estimates around $3 million). It was the home-based players, after all, who had got the show on the road.

The union insisted it had reached an in-principle agreement with Soccer Australia chief executive David Woolley shortly after the Tahiti match in Canberra. But when the squad assembled for the four nations tournament, the players discovered the deal had still not been ratified by Woolley's superiors. For those who had been around the team for awhile, it was a familiar story: empty promises. There was a

THE A/R/R/I/V/A/L

sinking feeling among the senior players that they were about to be ripped off once again.

But this time the players had the advantage of an organised union in their corner, and the benefit of a strong philosophical argument. If Soccer Australia was prepared to break the bank to employ Venables, why should the players miss out?

Venables sympathised. After all, in England he had been one of the driving forces behind the organisation of players' labour as far back as the 1960s. Yet he was reluctant to buy into the dispute. He didn't know enough of the background, and he would rather the union and his employers sorted it out. Realistically, in his first spell in charge, it was a mess he could have done without.

Once the players had settled into their Brisbane hotel, they were addressed by the union chief executive, Brendan Schwab, who had flown up from Melbourne late in the afternoon. At a previous meeting held just before the New Zealand game, the players had agreed to postpone any action in the hope that Soccer Australia would come to the bargaining table. But there had been no hint of a compromise in the meantime.

So the players decided it was time to take a stand. A vote was taken. By a majority of 21–1, it was agreed to embark on a campaign of industrial action. A strike for the final match of the series, against Norway in Sydney on the Saturday night, was left as a last resort. In the meantime the players reserved the right to boycott training sessions and to refuse to take part in any promotional activity on behalf of the federation. They were angry and disillusioned. They were tired of being treated as second-class citizens. They meant business.

When the story broke, Soccer Australia hastily attempted to gloss over the ramifications. A pugnacious Hill reiterated his stand that there would be no negotiating until the tournament was over. But the players knew from past experience that unless they made a stand while games were being played, their bargaining power would be drastically reduced. The team stood firm, and it won. But it was to prove a pyrrhic victory once again.

Woolley formally agreed to reopen discussions with the union in order to ensure the match against the Koreans went ahead. The players backed off in the spirit of cooperation. But as had so often been the case, that cooperation was not reciprocated. The games went ahead in good faith, but the players had been duped. Soccer Australia had succeeded with its delaying tactics. No agreement was to be reached during, or even shortly after, the tournament. In fact it was not until three months later that any substantive offer was put on the table, and by that stage the local players were not even in the room.

Against this difficult backdrop, the players could have been excused for having their minds elsewhere when they took the pitch at Lang Park. They could have been excused for a limp display against a Korean side in the first throes of rebuilding under new coach Cha Bum-kun. But after a pulsating, invigorating contest before over 15 000 fans, no excuses were needed. The Socceroos rose magnificently to the occasion.

On a hot, cloying evening, this was to be one of the finest Socceroo performances in memory. Not only was it a dramatic improvement on the uncertain effort against New Zealand four days before, but it was arguably the best result Venables would achieve right up until the World Cup play-offs later in the year.

South Korea showed the makings of an outstanding team that night, something they subsequently proved by qualifying comfortably for their fifth World Cup. But Venables' Australian side of part-timers took the game to the admirable Koreans, and won. And not just on the scoreboard. Significantly, the players also won themselves huge respect in the eyes of their new coach. If Venables had been privately concerned about a perceived gap in quality between the domestic players and the expatriates, he had come to realise that the locals weren't that far off the pace. Foster was outstanding, Bingley scored again, Trimboli and Trajanovski looked clever and inventive, while at the back the old guard of Ivanovic and Tobin rediscovered their best form.

And Venables emerged a big winner, too, in the minds of a discerning public. This was exactly the type of match that past Socceroo teams would have lost. They would have hesitated after going a goal up. They would have fallen in behind the ball. They would have retreated under the Korean onslaught in the second half. But not this time. The players slugged it out with their opponents toe-to-toe as play swept from one end of the pitch to the other. It was restless, it was energetic, it was exhilarating, it was a mighty spectacle. And to cap it off, the good guys won the game.

It was also a result which virtually guaranteed Venables a tournament at his first attempt. Even a draw in their final match against Norway would be good enough to secure the Socceroos their first trophy of any significance since 1985. The Norwegians, who were in a position to win the trophy themselves, were never going to lie down. Their long-ball, physical style remained a threat to any team in the world, even if they had left most of their best players behind. And Olsen would enjoy the chance to put one over his old rival, Venables, once again.

Previous page: Ned Zelic out jumps his opposite number, New Zealand's Mike McGarry.
CLAYTON/THE SYDNEY MORNING HERALD
Above: New Zealand's goalkeeper fails to prevent Craig Foster scoring Australia's third goal. CLAYTON/THE SYDNEY MORNING HERALD

Previous page: Australian socceroo Mark Viduka. CLAYTON/THE SYDNEY MORNING HERALD
Above: Terry Venables watching the Australian team training in preparation for the World Cup qualifying matches. CLAYTON/THE SYDNEY MORNING HERALD

T/H/E A/R/R/I/V/A/L

But not this time. The Socceroos adapted admirably to the challenge presented by Norway at the Sydney Football Stadium. A bruising game was ultimately settled by a single goal from Hooker. If Bingley was enjoying most of the accolades for his incisive bursts down the right flank, Hooker was determined to show he could do just as much damage down the left. The scoreboard flashed 1–0 to Australia and the silverware was hoisted above Tobin's ruffled head. In just over a week, Venables had performed wonders. But the recipe had been simple enough. By giving his players the support and belief they deserved, he was rewarded by the way they expressed themselves on the park.

After the game, at a press conference held in the SFS gymnasium, Venables was suitably enthused. 'They don't look like part-time players to me,' he said. 'We must not put ourselves down. Australian players are very good footballers and they have been a pleasure to work with.' The feeling, even at this embryonic stage, was mutual.

The following morning, with his own objective having been met, Venables flew to the Queensland resort of Hayman Island for a week-long holiday with his wife. The timing of the holiday was questionable, and drew sharp criticism from a media corps which had been lauding his achievements of the night before. In normal circumstances, the responsibilities of a national coach are not limited to what happens on the pitch. But Venables, clearly, was concerned primarily with the Socceroos. Television programs such as 'Sportsworld' and 'The Today Show' were told the coach was not available for a week. Club coaches who had been hoping to meet Venables were put off. Sponsors hoping for a speaking engagement were to be disappointed. It was not that Venables did not deserve a holiday; everyone did. But because he'd chosen to continue to live in London, he was only scheduled to be in the country for five weeks. Surely, then, he could have taken a break at a more opportune time?

'Terry made it clear he didn't want to be tugged left, right and centre by the media, or anyone else,' said Speziale. 'Taking that holiday definitely made life difficult for me. It was a golden opportunity to take the game to new audiences, and I would have loved to have fed that curiosity. But Terry's number one goal was to get things going with the team. He felt that had been achieved.'

Venables, however, was not completely out of contact on the Great Barrier Reef. He liaised regularly with Hill as attempts were made to arrange more matches in Europe during March and April. By the time he returned to Sydney, two fixtures—against Macedonia and Hungary—had been confirmed. And before he left Australia a few days later, Venables did make his services available for the cause. Functions were held in Wollongong, Adelaide and Perth on successive nights before Venables flew back to London, readying himself for the next stage of the Socceroo evolution. But before then, another matter would distract him. It would distract others as well. It was called Portsmouth Football Club. It looked a nice bit of business, too. But, then again, looks can often deceive.

CHAPTER 6

POMPEYROOS

Portsmouth Football Club. Founded 1898, now a century old. Affectionately known as 'Pompey'. Most successful period either side of World War II: an FA Cup victory in 1939 and two league championships in succession shortly after hostilities ended (1949 and 1950). Otherwise, not a lot to boast about, although for a long time Jimmy Dickinson proudly held the record for the number of English league appearances (764). That aside, Portsmouth have generally flattered to deceive. Fratton Park is scarcely regarded as a hotbed of English football. More like a sunbed, really, given the club's close proximity to the pebbled beaches of the English channel.

Perhaps that is what enticed Venables, who enjoys working on his tan. More likely, however, Portsmouth represented the chance to realise two of his enduring ambitions: ownership of a football club and the chance to make some money—serious money. One thing that has long been agreed upon is that Portsmouth are a club with enormous potential; the potential has been submerged, that's all.

Venables hoped to change all that, to awaken the sleeping giant. Others hoped for the same, not least the club's long-suffering supporters, who had last savoured top division football in the late 1980s—only to see a promising team dismembered when leading players such as Guy Whittingham, Kit Symons, John Beresford and Darren Anderton were sold off.

So when Venables arrived on the south coast shortly after Euro '96 as Pompey's 'director of football', the fans hoped the good times were on the way back. Fresh from taking England to the semifinals of the European Championships, Venables settled comfortably into the directors' box at Fratton Park. Terry Fenwick may have been the manager, but few doubted he would be relying heavily upon Venables for his advice.

But Portsmouth would not hold Venables' undivided attention. It was also at this time that the opportunity to coach the Socceroos surfaced. Right from the outset of his discussions with Hill, Venables made it clear he was not prepared to relinquish his newly acquired interest in Portsmouth. In the early stages, this interest was not financial, but Venables informed Hill that the situation could change. Hill, for his part, remained unconcerned. All he asked, in light of the controversy that had surrounded the final years of Thomson's reign, was that Venables not involve himself 'directly' in any negotiations to buy Australian players for his club.

Later, Hill readily confirmed the existence of just such a clause in the contract that Venables eventually signed with Soccer Australia. The new Socceroo coach was, understandably, happy to be offered such leeway. The clear implication from his new employers was that, aside from coaching the national team, he was free to do what he liked.

A week after he returned to England from his first sojourn as Socceroo coach, Venables took Hill at his word. He announced he had bought a 51 per cent shareholding in Portsmouth for the nominal fee of £1 from the former owner, Martin Gregory. The Gregory family had a long association with Venables. Martin's father, Jim, had been chairman of Queens Park Rangers during the 1970s when Venables enjoyed some of his best years as a player. Jim Gregory, however, was plagued with diabetes and had handed over control of the club to his son. Encouraged by his father's fondness for Venables, Martin decided to virtually give away control of Portsmouth to him. His belief was that Venables enjoyed such standing within the game that he would have little trouble attracting the sort of investment necessary to turn an ailing football club into a force, both on and off the pitch. 'The potential here is frightening,' Venables said upon his takeover. 'I plan to be here for awhile. Lots of changes have to be made but there is the basis of a great club here.'

Back in Australia, however, the alarm bells began to ring. Surely owning a professional club at the same time as coaching a national team constituted a conflict of interest situation? It was a view shared by many within the Australian game, but not by the man who counted—Hill. The day after the deal was announced, the chairman was sufficiently unmoved to say:

> 'When we initially negotiated the contract with Terry we were well aware he had a £1 option to buy Portsmouth. We didn't have any difficulties with that at the time, and we don't now. We have a view that it does not matter if the

national coach has a wide range of other interests, providing there are no conflicts of interest, and he would still have the ability to give 100 per cent to the Australian job.'

Hill reiterated that Venables had agreed to a clause prohibiting him from becoming involved in any way in the transfer of an Australian player to Portsmouth, including Australians already playing at other English or European clubs.

But less than a month later, history was to repeat itself. Just a few weeks after Venables took charge at Portsmouth, the club opened discussions with Socceroo goalkeeper Zeljko Kalac about a possible transfer to Fratton Park. Throughout their long history, Pompey had never had an Australian player on their books; not one. But suddenly Kalac was in their sights, and more Australians were to follow. When the news broke, Kalac admitted the obvious when he said it 'wouldn't look good' for Venables if he joined Portsmouth. 'I know questions will be asked, but at the end of the day it could be a good move for me,' Kalac said. His president at Sydney United, Ivan Simic, was equally sensitive to appearances. 'I would prefer to sell him to someone else, for the sake of Terry Venables and for the sake of Spider [Kalac]. It doesn't matter what they will say, people will still talk. I would think Venables needs a controversy like this like a hole in the head.' Soccer Australia's vice-chairman, Basil Scarsella, who had helped negotiate the terms of Venables' contract, was less forthcoming, but he too expressed reservations. 'Obviously, it would be preferable if Australian players didn't go to Portsmouth while Venables is in charge of the national team, but that doesn't necessarily mean it has to be avoided.'

And it wasn't. Two months later, Kalac concluded his transfer to Portsmouth for a fee worth $800 000 to cash-strapped Sydney United. There had been an eleventh-hour bid from rival English club West Ham, but the goalkeeper surprisingly resisted the temptation of stepping up a grade to the Premier League. Asked whether he had feared upsetting Venables if he'd chosen to go to Upton Park, Kalac replied, 'He didn't put any pressure on me at all. We didn't discuss it.' Sydney United teammate Robbie Enes, also included by Venables in the Socceroo squad, completed the same move to Portsmouth at the same time. West Adelaide's uncapped Hamilton Thorp duly made it an Aussie trifecta at Fratton Park.

All three deals were completed within a week. Officially the negotiations were finalised by Fenwick, who had arrived in Sydney 12 hours after Venables and who enjoyed easy access to the Socceroo squad in order to complete the signings. And Fenwick didn't stop there. By the time the opening round of qualifiers against

Tahiti and the Solomon Islands had been completed, two more Socceroos—John Aloisi and Craig Foster—had swelled Portsmouth's Antipodean contingent to five. And all of this, the hierarchy continued to insist, had been arranged without Venables becoming directly involved. 'Anyone's entitled to come here and look, and Portsmouth is no exception,' Venables told a press conference on the eve of the Superstars series, which preceded the World Cup campaign. 'I don't see it as a conflict of interest. If you see it that way, that's your business.'

The real business was that by the time Portsmouth opened the 1997/98 season, they had six Australians on their books, with young striker Paul Harries having been signed from the NSW Academy on the eve of the kick-off. There was genuine optimism among Pompey fans that with the influx of new talent and the more hands-on role adopted by Venables (by now installed as chairman), the club could mount a serious campaign for promotion to the Premier League. And in the early weeks, with Aloisi banging in a succession of vital goals, those hopes seemed justified. But then it all began to go terribly wrong.

Enes and Kalac were struggling to get work permits, and then Foster and Aloisi were called away on World Cup duty. So, too, were Portsmouth's two Jamaican internationals, Fitzroy Simpson and Paul Hall. The departures coincided with the team's inexorable slide down the table. The natives were getting restless, too. Work on a new grandstand, costing the equivalent of $6 million, was suspended a month into the season. Even before a ball had been kicked, the club had been late in paying players their pre-season wages. Rumours of serious financial problems began to grow, and in tandem with the sequence of poor results it was no surprise that the atmosphere around the town became poisonous. The local newspaper, the *News*, was banned by the club for its vigorous reporting. And the sharp end of Fleet Street started to ask questions. But Venables was proving a hard man to pin down for the answers.

As the Socceroos prepared for the decisive stage of their World Cup campaign, the matches against Iran, Venables found himself increasingly in a fix. His club was by now losing around $120 000 a week, and once again the players found their wages unpaid for the month of November. The union, the PFA, was called in for the second time, and Venables even pledged to help out with a loan if required. Ultimately, however, he didn't need to open his wallet.

After an investigation by *Daily Telegraph* journalist Mihir Bose, it emerged that Venables had been paid a handsome 'bonus' shortly after the combined $12 million sales of strikers Lee Bradbury and Deon Burton (to Manchester City and Derby

County respectively) on the eve of the new season. Bose was a bitter adversary of Venables, having written a series of damning articles following his acrimonious departure from Tottenham Hotspur four years previously. Now he revealed that Venables' company, Vencorp, had received $700 000 plus $110 000 VAT less than two weeks after the record sale of Bradbury. Given that the Portsmouth players were unpaid at the time, it was hardly a public relations triumph for Venables, despite his fierce denials that the timing of the bonus was coincidental. And trouble began to brew on a multitude of other fronts, as well.

The faith of the Gregory family in Venables' ability to entice new investment into Portsmouth—by now pulling only half the 16 000 fans needed each week just to break even—was diminishing rapidly. The family's growing scepticism was reflected in their refusal to sell Venables their 46 per cent of shares in the club. The reverse, in fact—Martin Gregory initiated moves to reclaim the shares that had been given to Venables. For his part, Venables suggested he might be willing to sell because he couldn't acquire full financial control of the club. Venables insisted he was unable to float Portsmouth on the stock market, as he had planned, because the Gregory family would not hand over the rest of their shares. As a consequence, Venables was unable to raise the $8.5 million needed to buy out the family, and his relations with Martin Gregory were becoming severely strained. 'I want someone to join me to help with the finances and help the club go forward,' Venables proclaimed. 'But if I cannot attract any investment, then I will have to listen to anything.' What he found himself listening to was a deafening silence. Venables was cornered, and the issue was how to find a way out.

Others were less concerned with Venables' financial woes, and more with the ethical question of Portsmouth's employment of so many Australians. The rumour mill wondered who was next. Socceroos Damian Mori and Robbie Slater became the latest names linked to a move to Fratton Park. Middlesbrough goalkeeper Mark Schwarzer weighed in with a stinging tirade—accusing Venables of having a pact with his Australian contingent at Portsmouth after he was left out of the World Cup squad. Schwarzer claimed he was amazed that conflict of interest allegations were dismissed so readily by Soccer Australia. 'They had an inquiry with Eddie Thomson for two and a half years, and when it's brought up regarding Terry Venables it's dismissed within a day or two,' Schwarzer said.

Former Socceroo Frank Farina sympathised. 'I certainly think there is a conflict of interest there, as does, I think, everyone else in Australia. Soccer Australia most probably knows as well as everyone that it doesn't just look like it—it is a conflict of interest.' In response to the growing outcry, the administration remained subdued. Yet by the time Venables returned to London after the devastating World Cup failure in Melbourne, doing nothing was less of an option. The stand-off at Portsmouth was reaching a climax.

Eight months after taking control at Fratton Park, Venables was facing the prospect that his dream of owning a successful football club was over. By now Martin Gregory was claiming publicly that Venables did not own the original 51 per cent because he had not lived up to his side of the bargain. In the same breath, it was announced that he was no longer the chairman. But just before he departed for Saudi Arabia to again take charge of the Socceroos, Venables insisted this was not the case. 'I got a letter last night to say the 51 per cent shareholding is not mine, which I find a bit strange,' he said. 'They are my shares, they are held by my bank. No-one has ever doubted that.' Effectively, however, the question was not whether he would be leaving Portsmouth, but when.

Venables began to consider his alternatives. While in Saudi Arabia for the Confederations Cup tournament, he was linked to the World Cup-bound Nigerian team, who at that stage were without a coach. South Africa was also touted as a possibility. Back in England, the noose was tightening. Brian Howe, the former lead singer with the band Bad Company, was aggressively promoting a bid to bail out Portsmouth as long as Venables was out of the club. 'Venables has been impossible to deal with,' said Howe. 'We e-mail him, and he replies back at snail-mail speed. Mr Gregory has been very businesslike.' Howe, a lifelong Pompey fan, was negotiating a takeover in partnership with billionaire American sports stadium developer Vince Wolanin. The promise was for a massive injection of fresh capital, around $250 million, including a new stadium. The Gregory family was keener than ever to listen.

So too, it seemed, were many of the players and fans. For the first time the constituency which Venables had regarded as his own began to turn against him. Striker John Durnin, the club's PFA representative, said: 'Without being disrespectful to Mr Venables, who is a very high-profile man in football, I think the players can concentrate better when he is not around. The club seems to run a lot smoother, and I think the gaffer [Fenwick] finds it a lot easier. He can be a distraction.' The club's no. 1 fan, who had changed his name by deed poll to John Mr Portsmouth Football Club Westwood, was equally disillusioned. Westwood told the *Guardian* newspaper: 'The signing of Terry Venables was another smokescreen to keep down demonstrations from fans. Now, after hearing of his £300 000 performance bonus, even those who applauded his appointment believe he's rooked us. When he came, he said that if there came a time when Portsmouth didn't want him, he would walk away. So why is he now fighting tooth and nail to remain chairman? I would like to see him, Gregory and Fenwick go. The fans are fed up with politics. We just want a football team to watch on Saturdays.'

By the time Venables returned from Socceroo duty in Riyadh, Pompey were occupying the basement of the first division. Indeed Christmas 1997 was not a time of good cheer for the usually affable Cockney. The Socceroos had just missed out on the World Cup; Nigeria had given the coaching job to someone else; South Africa, also in the market for a new man for France 98, chose a Frenchman; and Portsmouth were falling apart at the seams. To cap it off, Venables was facing two crucial legal decisions early in the New Year. The Premier League's 'bung inquiry' would announce whether he had a case to answer, while the Department of Trade and Industry (DTI) was to decide on a series of charges relating to his fitness to be a company director.

The good news came from the bung inquiry. While the inquiry had found that Venables' conduct in the 1992 transfer of Teddy Sheringham from Nottingham Forest to Tottenham 'cannot be justified', the Football Association subsequently decided to take no action. Elsewhere, however, a dark cloud gathered on the horizon.

The DTI succeeded, by some margin, in its High Court attempt to have Venables disqualifed as a company director. Venables accepted 19 DTI charges of serious misconduct—many of them relating to his time at Tottenham—and agreed to pay costs, estimated to be $1.2 million. Among the allegations Venables did not dispute in court were that he had dishonestly borrowed $2.2 million to help buy a share of Tottenham, and that he had used his long-time adviser Eddie Ashby to take part directly in the management of Tottenham and Scribes at a time when Ashby was an undischarged bankrupt. The High Court ruled that Venables was to be banned from holding any directorship for seven years—a suspension that will not expire until 2005.

Perhaps sensing what was to come, Venables finally stood down as chairman of Portsmouth on the eve of the DTI hearing. He was reportedly paid around $450 000 for his disputed shareholding, about half of what he had initially demanded for walking away. So despite the humbling experience, Venables was to eventually leave Fratton Park with a handsome profit from his brief and stormy tenure.

'He came here as the greatest thing since sliced bread,' said reporter Simon Parker of the *News*. 'But he was hardly ever on the training ground. He became

Venables the businessman, not Venables the football coach. The club got dragged through the headlines for all the wrong reasons. When he went, there was basically a sense of relief.'

A few days after Venables' exit, it was hardly a surprise when Kalac announced he would not be pursuing his intended move to Portsmouth. The transfer had been delayed for months by work permit problems, but when Venables walked out the door—taking Fenwick with him—Kalac decided it might be better to sit tight at Sydney United.

For the Australians who had jumped in at the start—Aloisi, Foster, Enes and Thorp—the task was to pick up the pieces. Aloisi suddenly found himself out of the team despite being the club's top scorer. The Socceroo striker claimed that Alan Ball, who had replaced Fenwick as manager, was overlooking the Aussie contingent in a reaction to Venables' departure.

For the author of the official Portsmouth Centenary Pictorial History there was a different kind of challenge. Peter Jeffs had to arrange a reprint of thousands of copies at the last minute in order to remove a picture of a beaming Venables from the front cover.

Unquestionably, the episode had been nothing less than a disaster. One month after Venables left, the club revealed losses of $4.9 million for the 12 months until May 1997. Portsmouth were continuing to lose an estimated $260 000 per week. 'It is no secret that the dispute with Mr Venables severely affected our financial stability,' claimed a directors' statement. 'Fortunately it has now been settled, and we can plan for the future. We believe that we will now all be pulling in the same direction with the wellbeing of Portsmouth Football Club as our only concern.'

Venables angrily deflected the blame, saying, 'They're crying like babies now that it's going wrong. They wanted to sell the club to somebody in America and when that fell through they ended up with egg on their face.'

Whatever the case, a chapter has closed. And for Venables, a business career which began at the age of 18 will be hard to kick-start. By the time he is able to take an active role again he will be 62—a late start for someone intending to build a financial empire. Venables conceded as much after the DTI ruling. 'The business side is something I had to get out of my system,' he said. 'I have paid the price, a heavy one, and I regret that. But I do not regret having tried to make a go of it.' His future, clearly, belonged on the pitch. This was an argument that had been put to him many times by friends and associates. It was an argument he finally felt compelled to accept.

CHAPTER 7

THE FOREIGN LEGION

TERRY VENABLES THOUGHT LONG AND HARD about it. He had been pleasantly surprised by both the quality and quantity of Australia's home-based players during the recent four nations series. The domestic players had certainly done their candidacy no harm at all. So he contemplated changing his plans; he wondered whether he should reward them with continued selection. It was a tough call, but after deliberating Venables decided to stick with Plan A.

It had taken a lot of difficult negotiation to secure two games in Europe for the Socceroos. The purpose of the games in Skopje and then Budapest had, all along, been to offer a shop window for his impressive collection of overseas-based professionals. After all, these were the players who had attracted him to the job in the first place. These were the players everyone believed would form the nucleus of Australia's World Cup side. The locals had made him think twice, but his gut feeling was that it was time to see what the fuss was about.

The matches against the former Yugoslav Republic of Macedonia and Hungary would, therefore, be exclusively the domain of the foreign legion. The big names. The stars. The players who would whet the appetite of any self-respecting coach, anywhere in the world. As a coach accustomed to working with the best, Venables was eager to see how this lot stacked up.

The failure to secure a match against Croatia, set down for Rijeka in late February, had thrown something of a spanner into the works. The Croatians were certainly a pedigree team, and would give the Socceroos a serious workout. It was somewhat ironic, then, that the game was postponed because the Croatians were fearful of the consequences of not fielding their own full-strength side. Croatian officials had come to appreciate the standard of the Australian game over recent years. There were a handful of Australians, all of Croatian heritage, playing successfully in their own league. There were Croatian coaches such as Josef Kuze, Dom Kapetanovic and Vedran Rozic who all boasted experience in Australia's national league. And five years earlier, the Croatian federation had handed Australia the compliment of selecting it as the venue for the first-ever overseas tour by its national team. The Croatians had expected a comfortable ride, but returned home with two losses and a draw against an under-strength Socceroo team. For all those reasons, Croatian officials were loathe to take on Venables' squad unless they could guarantee the appearance of their best players, such as Boban, Suker, Boksic, Bilic and Prosinecki. When they found they couldn't, the decision was made to call off the game. A compliment to the Australians, no question.

Another compliment was issued by FIFA shortly afterwards. In its February world rankings, FIFA promoted the Socceroos 17 places to a record high of 33rd. It was 11 places higher than the best ranking achieved by Thomson, and a direct consequence of the efforts of the home-based players in beating both Norway and South Korea a month earlier.

'Australia is going to be taken a lot more seriously in future,' said Soccer Australia chairman David Hill. Venables was treating the Socceroos seriously, too. After sifting through a list of some 70 potential candidates, he announced a 29-man squad for a training camp in London, scheduled to replace the postponed Croatia game. From the camp, the numbers would be whittled down for the friendlies against Macedonia and Hungary. Four uncapped players were selected, headed by youngsters John Aloisi and Josip Skoko. As an indication of how far and wide Australia's overseas talent was spread, players from clubs in 11 different countries converged on Ealing in north London. It was a major event in itself.

Five television stations, including American cable network CNN, sent crews to the first training session. All the major English papers were there, not surprisingly given Venables' long and intimate relationship with Fleet Street. Leeds United manager George Graham, one of Venables' oldest friends in football, also showed up, along with a host of scouts from various clubs.

Mehmet Durakovic, who had flown halfway across the world from Malaysia, was taken aback by the level of interest. 'Obviously Terry is a big name, but I was still surprised at how many media people were there, how much of a big deal it was

THE FOREIGN LEGION

in England,' he said. 'We actually used the official England team bus to get to the training ground, so maybe people had us confused with them. I don't know. But it was an exciting atmosphere, even for someone who had been around the team as long as me.'

The camp dovetailed nicely with Durakovic's club commitments with Selangor, who, under new coach Steve Wicks (once a player under Venables at Queens Park Rangers), had decided to use England for a pre-season tour. Two other Asian-based players, Graham Arnold and Tony Popovic, were not so fortunate. Their new Japanese club, Sanfrecce Hiroshima, was paying them a handsome salary and wanted them to stay and prepare for the new season instead. Both players were also carrying niggling injuries. Other injured players did show up, primarily because they didn't have far to travel. Carl Veart, Jason van Blerk and Lucas Neill were all playing for London clubs, and were invited along to meet the new boss, despite being unable to train.

Even for hardened veterans like Durakovic there was a sense of awe in meeting Venables for the first time. 'I'd heard about him all my life, so it was a big thrill, and honour, to shake hands with him,' he said. 'There was definitely a difference from before. I mean all of us had known Thommo (Eddie Thomson) for a fair while, so I guess there was a familiarity there. But with Terry you felt a little bit nervous, a little bit unsure. It was like starting all over again. And he was very professional about it all. All the boys were pretty impressed.'

Those feelings were echoed by Robbie Slater and Mark Bosnich. 'I've been involved with the Socceroos for 10 years now and it was totally different,' Slater said. 'His influence is just the respect the man gets. He was a great player in his time, he's a great manager and you can see by the little things he says that he makes sense of the game.' Bosnich added to the *Sydney Morning Herald*: 'I hope it provides stiff competition, because the more competition there is the harder people will push themselves, and the more people push themselves the better it is for Australia.'

There was competition, all right. Venables' task for the three-day camp was clearly defined. The formalities were to introduce himself, and to explain his own plans and what he wanted from the players in the build-up to the World Cup campaign. But the pressing priority was to whittle the numbers down for the match against Macedonia, to be played a fortnight later. The home-based players had staked to their claims during the four nations tournament in January; now it was the turn of the high-profile expatriates to show they deserved the inside running.

Missing from the list of 18 players selected for the trip to the Balkans were

Thomson favourites such as Andrew Bernal, Jason van Blerk and Paul Agostino. Venables preferred to go for youth instead, promoting uncapped youngsters John Aloisi and Josip Skoko, and retaining Harry Kewell and Lucas Neill, who had both seen limited action towards the end of the Thomson reign. The selection of Aloisi, at that stage playing in Italy's second division with Cremonese, was particularly interesting. Aloisi had fallen out badly with national assistant coach Les Scheinflug three years earlier over his refusal to travel to Fiji to play for the Australian youth team. He was playing in Belgium at the time. In the aftermath, he sent a letter to Soccer Australia announcing he did not wish to be considered for future selection, effectively 'retiring' from the national team at the age of 18. But as his club career took an upswing following his move to Italy—he became the first Australian to score in the *Serie A*—many hoped the impasse could be overcome. But it needed a change of coach to provide the catalyst. Right from the start, Venables made it clear that he considered the pacey, athletic striker as part of his plans. Aloisi responded by ending his self-imposed exile, and in Macedonia he returned to the fold.

On the subject of the younger brigade, Venables said: 'I'm a believer in the theory that if you're good enough, you're old enough. All these lads impressed me during the camp. How are they going to get experience if you don't put them in?' The experience was almost over before it began. The Macedonian federation had scheduled the game for Bitola, a small market town in the south of the country, close to the Greek border. But after an inspection by a Soccer Australia representative, Venables vetoed the choice of location. The stadium lacked adequate facilities and the pitch was in poor condition. The Socceroos would not play, he said, unless the match was switched to the national stadium in the capital, Skopje. After a stalemate which lasted three days, the Macedonians relented. The match was important for their own preparation for upcoming World Cup fixtures, and they didn't want it cancelled at the last moment. Coach Djoko Hadjilevski had enough problems already, with five of the country's leading players, among them striker Darko Pancev, boycotting the national team. His predecessor as national coach, Andon Doncevksi, claimed that without the five players—all playing abroad—the Macedonians would be in trouble against Australia. 'The Socceroos now play like a strong European team. I think they will win,' he said.

The Australian players flew into Skopje just two days before the match, but goalkeeper Mark Schwarzer was not among them. Schwarzer withdrew from the squad to remain in England and help Middlesbrough in their twin ambitions of

THE FOREIGN LEGION

avoiding relegation from the Premier League and winning the League Cup. It was a decision that was to cost him dearly. Both Venables and his assistant, Blanco, had placed a high premium on commitment to the cause. Players who pulled out of matches were not to be forgiven lightly. Schwarzer, more than anyone, was to pay the price. At their hotel in Skopje, the players were called to a meeting and reminded again of their obligations.

'Basically he told us that our first priority for the rest of the year had to be to Australia,' recalled Durakovic. 'He really drilled that into us. He said the boys in Australia had done well, and now it was up to us. The door was open for everyone, but he wanted us to commit ourselves.'

On the eve of the game, another player, Craig Moore, withdrew after claiming he had missed a connecting flight in London. Steve Horvat got a reprieve in a late reshuffle. But despite the interruptions to his planning, Venables still had the luxury of fielding a decent side at the Gradski Stadium. Australia's strength in depth was coming to the fore.

On a sunny afternoon, the stadium was less than one-third full for the first-ever international between the two nations. A pitch which was bumpy in patches but soft underneath caused some anxious moments early on for the Socceroos, but as the match wore on they gradually played their way into form. The Macedonians looked threatening on the break, and but for a fine reflex save by Bosnich to deny Dzevded Stainovski, the home side may well have gone ahead. But the Australian defence galvanised, and the midfield began to look more composed with Slater shifting from the flank into a central role. Yet it was a generally uninspiring encounter, and the match seemed destined for a scoreless draw until skipper for the day Aurelio Vidmar intervened decisively in the dying moments. A cross from substitute Danny Tiatto drifted invitingly into his path, and Vidmar dispatched his header with typical precision. It was the second time Vidmar had captained his country, and the second time he had won the game with the only goal. Given his tribulations at club level with his Spanish side Tenerife, Vidmar clearly relished the return to international duty.

There was little time to celebrate. The players went straight back to their hotel, packed, and flew out of Skopje later that night. But they took with them the satisfaction of having delivered an encouraging result for the new coach, who now boasted the impressive record of four wins out of four. Just as importantly, they had made their case a strong one. 'Both the boys in Australia and here have given me some problems to think about, but they are good problems to have,' Venables told reporters after the game.

The competition for places, certainly, was hotting up. The expatriates had one more opportunity to make their claims before the World Cup squad was decided. Australia had been invited to Hungary for a match to coincide with the 75th birthday of Hungary's most famous footballer, Ferenc Puskas. It was to be a festive occasion, attended by FIFA's president, Joao Havelange, no less. Puskas also had a connection with Australia, something not generally known to his many friends in Europe. The Mighty Magyar had spent three years coaching South Melbourne during the early 1990s—his stay highlighted by winning the championship in 1991. Puskas was delighted that the Socceroos would be there to celebrate his birthday at the Nepstadion.

Venables, however, had no time to party. Again his dilemma was how to squeeze all the credible candidates into an 18-man squad. In the event, he decided to make four changes, bringing in Graham Arnold and Tony Popovic from Japan, and Kevin Muscat and Stan Lazaridis from England. Schwarzer and Moore, the late withdrawals from Skopje, had to pay their penance and were overlooked. Again there was a late absentee, Damien Mori, but he had an excuse that Venables was prepared to accept. Mori pulled out of the Hungary match because his wife was about to give birth to their first baby.

No-one was more thrilled to win selection than Arnold. With his career approaching its twilight, he had pondered whether he would get a chance under a new coach. When he was told he had been picked he was delighted, not least because the match in Budapest would also mark his 50th appearance for his country—a fresh start and a personal milestone into the bargain. Even better, Arnold was selected to start.

Again the players arrived late from their various destinations, with the full squad only coming together 48 hours before the kick-off for a light training run at the Ferencvaros Stadium. Again Venables was quick to seek out the newcomers and make them feel welcome.

'It was a good first impression for me,' said Arnold. 'I noticed straightaway how relaxed, how in control, he was. Maybe the players weren't as jovial as normal, but that's because they were still finding their feet. Terry liked to be one of the boys, but as soon as we started training he would walk away to be by himself. I liked his style straightaway.'

That style was to spend time talking to players individually, making sure they felt comfortable with what the coach required of them. For most of them, it was

THE FOREIGN LEGION

different to what they were used to. Even the pep talk before the match was a surprise to Arnold. 'I think Terry talked for maybe three minutes,' he said. 'I couldn't believe it.'

A good-sized crowd had converged on the Nepstadion to honour Puskas, with highlights of his playing career shown on the big screen in the hour before the game got underway. The great man himself strolled out onto the pitch for a ceremonial kick-off, and had a word to both Arnold and Slater—whom he knew from his time in Australia—on the way back to the sideline. Puskas also knew something most of the crowd, and probably the Hungarian players, did not: the Socceroos were a decent team.

Vidmar, again, was quick to make the point. Six minutes gone and his header put the visitors in front. The home side equalised late in the first half, when they were enjoying their best spell of the game. As in Skopje, the game seemed headed for a draw. But again, as in Skopje, the Socceroos stung their opponents at the death. Vidmar scored again to put Australia in front, and substitute Kevin Muscat thrashed home his shot in injury time to put a gloss to the scoreline: 3–1 Australia. The local fans booed their team off the park. Venables could afford to smile. Five out of five. And more players had impressed. None more than Zelic, who had made a triumphant return to form. All agreed this was his best match in a green and gold shirt since his goal put Australia into the Barcelona Olympics five years before. Injury, strange career decisions and some serious self-analysis had stymied his progress. But in Budapest he was the Zelic of old, and Australia looked a far better team because of it.

Back at the hotel that night, Venables called the team into a meeting and toasted Arnold for his 50th cap. The players were certainly in a jovial mood. But there was some important business to attend to before the celebrations could get underway. David Hill stood up and announced to the players that he was now offering a new pay deal on behalf of Soccer Australia. This was the end result of the dispute that had threatened to sabotage the four nations tournament in January. The campaign for better guarantees had been organised and led by the home-based players, but Hill chose to make the offer first to the expatriates. Forms were handed around the room outlining the structure of the deal. Bosnich stood up and asked if it was negotiable. 'No, not really,' replied the chairman. So that was that—take it or leave it.

It was a typical Hill ultimatum. Given the background and length of the dispute, it could have been expected that a process of negotiation would take place. But the locals did not even know a deal was in the offing. In fact they knew nothing about it at all until the news was leaked in the newspapers a few days after the match in Budapest. To add salt to the wounds, at that point seven of the home-based players, including captain Alex Tobin, were still waiting on full payment for their four nations efforts three months earlier.

Players' union chief executive Brendan Schwab was, not surprisingly, outraged. 'This is an offer which has been made behind the backs of the union, and the domestic players, who are all members of the union,' Schwab said. 'The way it has been handled suggests they want to drive a wedge between the overseas players and the domestic players, and that's disappointing.' Hill was unmoved. 'Personally, I don't give a stuff about the union,' he said.

The reality was, of course, that Soccer Australia was in the driving seat. Months later Schwab would concede that the offer matched what the union had set out to achieve. The union's position was that while Soccer Australia may have been confrontational, what mattered most was that the players got what they deserved in the end. On paper, it certainly seemed to be a reasonable offer. 'This is the best anyone has ever got for playing for Australia,' Hill proclaimed. And he was right. For a player who figured regularly in Venables' plans, up to $70 000 in wages and bonuses could be earned in the 18 months leading up to and including the World Cup finals in France. In truth, it wasn't a bad earner.

The players, and their coach, had begun to show they were worth every penny. Victory in Budapest made it 100 per cent for Venables. What's more, the team had scored freely and entertained. The locals had made a mockery out of suggestions they would find it impossible to get into the World Cup squad. The expatriates had proved they were equal to the challenge. Winning was becoming a habit, and it was a good habit to get into. The mood was optimistic, the confidence growing with every outing. It was infectious.

'This is a team that can really go places,' said Aurelio Vidmar. 'What I like about Venables is that when he talks, he talks about going forward. We've got the mentality to go out there and win games. For me, this is the best squad we've ever had.'

CHAPTER 8

TALES FROM OCEANIA

SO THIS WAS THE WORLD CUP! Swaying palms; white sandy beaches; outrigger canoes; the sea a deep, cobalt blue; the sun; the smiles—paradise on earth, perhaps the last place to truly escape. Ask Gauguin. Ask Marlon Brando. Ask anyone who has been to Bora Bora, to Club Med.

In this vast, underpopulated region stretching from Australia to South America, organised sport often remains a contradiction in terms. And if there is some serious football to be played, it is usually the oval-balled variety. Rugby Union rules in the major island nations of Fiji, Tonga and Western Samoa. It is a game which suits the big, raw-boned population, a warrior-like people who can identify with the heavy body contact so fundamental to the 15-a-side game.

But the most popular sport on earth also enjoys a toehold in the South Pacific. Soccer is a favoured pastime of the Francophiles in Tahiti and New Caledonia, of the Indian minority in Fiji, and of the slightly built peoples of the Solomon Islands and Vanuatu. There are, indeed, enough soccer players in Oceania to give it a voice in FIFA's Zurich boardroom. And because of this, Oceania is where Australia's quest for the holy grail—a place in the World Cup—always begins.

Having fine-tuned the team in Skopje and Budapest, Venables was ready and willing for the opening stage of the Socceroos' World Cup campaign. He knew little about his prospective opponents, but then he didn't feel the need to know that much.

The way the system was to work was that the smaller island nations would play each other in preliminary rounds before joining the seeded nations of Australia, New Zealand, Fiji and Tahiti in the main draw. Given that the Socceroos remained supremely confident about beating New Zealand, theoretically the best of the rest in Oceania, any other opponent was sure to offer only a token threat to the best team Australia had ever had.

Venables, certainly, was well aware of just how good he had it. To get to the World Cup finals in France, the Socceroos would need to play eight games in total, six of them at home. And the first stage of four games would be the easiest. Australia was paired with Tahiti and the winner of the Melanesian/Polynesian play-off. As it happened, that winner turned out to be the Solomon Islands. Australia, Tahiti, the Solomons—exactly the same scenario as the last World Cup campaign in 1993.

But there was one important difference. Four years earlier, the Socceroos had been required to travel to Papeete and Honiara. This time around, all the games were to be hosted by the Socceroos at Parramatta Stadium. So Venables didn't need to do much homework. It wasn't sloppy planning, it was just plain fact. If there was still such a thing as a dead certainty in international football, this was it. The Socceroos would win Oceania Group One in a canter.

This lop-sided playing field continued to irritate Hill, whose campaign to extricate Australia from Oceania had reached a head the previous year.

The Oceania Football Confederation (OFC) had been founded by an Australian, Sir William Walkley, in 1966. In the ensuing years it was treated as little more than a nuisance by FIFA which, in all honestly, didn't know what to do with its least developed and least successful confederation. Australia, quite clearly, were too good for Oceania. FIFA knew this but couldn't, or wouldn't, do anything about it. So the OFC ambled on, short of money, short of ideas and short of friends. FIFA put it in the 'too-hard basket' at successive congresses in 1990 and 1994 despite, on both occasions, having suggested that the long-term future of the OFC would be addressed.

The catalyst for definitive action came when FIFA's president, Joao Havelange, announced, at the end of 1995, that he would be stepping down at France 98. The various contenders for the most powerful post in world sport suddenly realised that the previously unwanted OFC and its 10 precious votes could be of use. Promises were made. On one side, Sweden's Lennart Johansson was telling Hill he was ready to accommodate his obvious concerns that Australia needed a way out of Oceania. On the other side, the long-standing OFC president, Charlie Dempsey, was brokering a deal with Havelange, saying he would support plans to annoint a successor in return for formal recognition of the OFC.

Hill attempted to rally support by sending letters to 172 of the football world's 173 nations, outlining why Oceania was fundamentally flawed, why it was holding back Australia's development, and why formal recognition should be delayed once again until some form of compromise could be reached. It was an unprecedented, and clearly provocative, move. Not surprisingly, it earned Australia the wrath of the other nine members of the OFC.

Ultimately, Dempsey prevailed, with Hill humiliated on the floor of the FIFA Congress in Zurich. The vote was 172 for, one against. Thirty years after it was formed, the OFC had finally received a formal vote at the FIFA executive, and the rights and privileges of the other five confederations. What this meant, in essence, was that FIFA would start giving Oceania a decent slice of a pie that had been dramatically increased by television revenue.

The bottom line read well: $1 million to each Oceania nation, access to funds, and more support in terms of infrastructure and coaching. It was all Dempsey had hoped for, and more.

But Hill was not in the mood to be magnanimous. In a subsequent newspaper interview he likened Dempsey to the rag-and-bone character Albert Steptoe, of British television fame. Dempsey and the OFC executive were outraged. Hill was suspended from attending Oceania meetings and relations between the confederation and its strongest member nation reached their lowest ebb.

In truth, Hill possessed a sound argument. Few could dispute that it would take a long time for Oceania to provide Australia with worthwhile competition. But what Hill failed to appreciate fully was that geographically and politically Australia was left with no alternative. The Socceroos were stuck in Oceania and the best option was to make do.

Venables, for one, wasn't complaining. Without question, he had the easiest qualifying path to the World Cup finals for any nation, anywhere. If football politics meant Australia's high-profile professionals would have to share the same park with the amateurs of Tahiti and the Solomons, then so be it. Venables would happily accommodate the island minnows if it was to make life easier for the Socceroos. Which it did.

But first things first. Venables still had to find the right mix of local and overseas players, and as luck would have it there was the opportunity for one last selection trial before World Cup points were at stake. The second annual Superstars series was scheduled between the end of the domestic national league season and the

Oceania qualifiers. Two games, in Sydney and Melbourne, would give Venables the chance to make up his mind.

The Superstars series was the creation of Soccer Australia commissioner George Negus, who the year before had succeeded in selling his concept to Channel Nine. The made-for-TV spectacle would, Negus argued, enable soccer to test its market in commercial television. It would also provide a platform to showcase the talents of the overseas players—most of whom were out of sight and out of mind for much of the year.

In theory, it was a worthy idea. In reality, it was extremely difficult to put into practice. At least the 1996 series had boasted the attraction of providing a contest between local and overseas players. But this time around, with the need to build team spirit for the forthcoming World Cup games paramount in the equation, Venables made it clear he did not want to promote that particular rivalry.

Venables announced a list of 33 players for the Superstars series in early May. To the surprise of those who believed the World Cup squad would be dominated by the foreign legion, he had kept faith with a large contingent of locals. As Venables announced his Superstars squads via a video link-up from London, 13 local players remained in the frame. It was up to them to make the most of the opportunity.

'This is not a glorified training session, I can assure you,' Venables told the gathering. 'It's all about competition within the group. First, the players are aiming to survive when we have to make the decision of reducing the squad. Then it's about forcing your way into the team. And then it's about staying there.'

Not everyone saw the series as having such importance. By the time the opening game between Australia Green and Australia Gold kicked off before barely 2000 drenched fans at Olympic Park in Melbourne, a total of 12 players from the original list had pulled out. Ironically, two of the absentees, Arnold and Popovic, had been blocked from coming home by their coach—Eddie Thomson.

Venables remained, publicly at least, unperturbed by the spate of withdrawals. 'It doesn't bother me too much,' he said. 'The games are perfect for the Australian-based players, coming at the end of their season. We always knew there would be a problem with some of the European-based players.'

Venables flew into Australia a week before the series opened, to watch the national league grand final and to film a television advertisement for a British soft drink. The ad was filmed on an outback set near Broken Hill, and was later to cause some hand-wringing within the Australian game when it was aired. Venables was said to have been patronising towards Australian soccer, but Hill, quite rightly, said the only people upset by the ad were those without a sense of humour.

But the ad did have one costly effect. The soft drink promoted by Venables was a Schweppes product, and the Socceroos—at that point—were sponsored by a rival drink company, Coca Cola. Shortly afterwards, Coke withdrew their major sponsorship of the national team.

A few days after the filming, Venables was among the record crowd of 40 466 that saw the Brisbane Strikers clinch Queensland's first national championship in the grand final against Sydney United. The questions most asked of Venables inside the ground were these: Why couldn't the best club in the country get a single player in the national team? And why couldn't the Strikers even get a player selected in the froth-and-bubble Superstars series. Venables smiled a lot, but couldn't give the Queenslanders the answer they wanted to hear.

The only Brisbane presence when the Superstars kicked off in Melbourne was player/coach Frank Farina, and he was in the commentary box. Judging by the standard of the match played before him, Farina would not have looked out of place on the pitch. A low-key game ended in a 2–2 draw, and even Venables would have found it hard to glean anything useful out of the exercise. The only pleasing aspect was that nobody got hurt.

Seven days later, at Parramatta Stadium, the two teams met again. By this time a couple of reinforcements had drifted in. Moore, freshly wed, and Muscat, fresh from winning promotion to the Premier League with Crystal Palace, arrived from London. Channel Nine, having assessed the viewing figures from the first match, sensed the mood of general indifference. Originally scheduled to go out in prime time, the match was eventually broadcast at five minutes to midnight.

For all that, a surprising number of fans did show up at the ground. Almost 9000 were in attendance to see another draw, but this time they at least got something to shout about. Just before half-time, referee Brett Hugo sent off Damien Mori for a second bookable offence. It may have been the technically correct decision, but it was certainly not within the spirit of the match. Venables made his views clear by insisting that Mori be replaced, while the player was left to reflect on whether the refereeing aberration would cost him a place in the World Cup squad. He needn't have worried.

Two days after the second Superstars match, Venables showed his hand. But not as forcibly as had been expected. Having used almost 40 players during his six months in charge, it was anticipated he would reduce his World Cup squad to the official limit of 18; in other words, cut his list of candidates in half. What Venables did, instead, was announce a squad of 26 players to be kept together for the whole six weeks of the Oceania section of the campaign. There were only a few unhappy players, then, on the morning of 6 June. Thomson favourites such as Bernal, Kulcsar, Tiatto and van Blerk had reason to be disappointed. But otherwise, there were still plenty of shirts to go around. One jersey, however, was left on the hook.

The Australian media had rarely seen Venables as animated as he was on the subject of Mark Viduka's enforced absence from his first World Cup squad. Viduka had been picked for the Superstars series but had not shown up. He was then picked in the squad for the World Cup qualifiers, but the night before the squad was made public he again opted out. The player claimed he wanted to come home, but his club, Croatia Zagreb, did not want to release him. There was added speculation that Viduka had been called to a meeting at the home of the Croatian president, Franjo Tudjman, and told his priority was to have a rest and be ready for the new season with his club.

Whatever the case, Venables did not like what he was hearing. 'There has been a lot of pressure on Mark not to come, and I find that totally outrageous,' he said. 'It is not only a hefty kick in the teeth for Australia, but for Mark as well.' Strong words, and for Venables a rare public outburst. Comments that came from the heart. Comments that, months later, were to have sinister repercussions.

So it was a Viduka-less squad that assembled at the Parramatta Parkroyal Hotel in the second weekend of June. It was the start of the road to the World Cup, but France was a long way off. For now, it was time to focus on the task at hand: four games, two against Tahiti and two against the Solomon Islands, who had qualified by a circuitous route which involved a play-off against Tonga. Easy pickings, true enough. But the games had to be won all the same.

For the opposition, the objective was to beat each other. Neither Solomons coach Eddie Ngava or his Tahitian counterpart Richard Vansam seriously considered the possibility of beating the Socceroos. But these two nations had developed a healthy rivalry over the years, most of it played out in the South Pacific Games, and each felt it was important to avoid finishing bottom of the group.

Tahiti's hopes were not helped by a changing of the guard in their administration just three weeks before the qualifying series. As a result of the political machinations in Papeete, the squad arrived in Australia without having played a match in eight months, having had only four training sessions together, and without 75 per cent of their leading players, none of whom had been prepared to take the necessary time off work.

TALES FROM OCEANIA

The Solomons, the first-up opponents for Australia, looked to be in better shape. In the previous six months they had played four World Cup qualifiers and two friendly internationals against Vanuatu. The feeling was they would provide the Socceroos with their toughest opposition in the first game of the qualifying series.

As it transpired, nothing could have been further from the truth. Game one for Australia in the World Cup campaign of 1997 didn't just break the record book, it smashed it to pieces. The scoreline of 13–0 was the biggest in Australia's history. Aloisi and Mori celebrated the occasion with five goals each. And to put salt into the wound, Bosnich sprinted up the park to take and convert a penalty in the dying minutes, thereby becoming the first goalkeeper to score for the national team.

Overwhelmed and under-manned by the dismissal early in the second half of defender Daudau, the Solomons were hopelessly exposed. Basically, it was an embarrassment. It may have been the perfect start for Australia, but it was going to be hard for Venables to keep his players interested after this. The public was having a similar problem—just over 3000 fans showed up. For the turnstile operators, things were going to go from bad to worse.

Two nights later against Tahiti, there were expectations that the Socceroos could even surpass their amazing goal-scoring frenzy against the Solomons. But Venables continued to change his team around, making nine changes to the starting XI, and the lack of cohesion showed. Against a Tahitian team which played with just one striker and concentrated on getting bodies behind the ball, the Socceroos were contained to a 5–0 scoreline. Disappointed with five goals? It showed just how far the national team had come.

What the result did achieve was to all but guarantee Australia would win the group and advance to the Oceania play-offs. Amid the critical self-analysis, this very important point seemed to have been overlooked. Barring a miracle, the Socceroos had achieved what they had set out to do, which, after all, is what counts.

What counted for Tahiti and the Solomons was to win against each other, and in so doing avoid the dreaded bottom spot in the group. So while the Socceroos rested over the weekend, having played two matches in three days, the two island nations met each other to settle the score. In the unlikely venue of Gabbie Stadium, a modest ground situated in Sydney's north-western suburbs, just 253 paying spectators showed up on a bitterly cold afternoon to see history being made. Four days after their 13-goal beating at the hands of the Socceroos, the Solomons salvaged some pride with a 4–1 win over Tahiti—their first victory against their old rivals in

15 meetings. The players celebrated as if they had won the World Cup!

For Australia, too, there was a special reason to celebrate when they resumed their campaign against the Solomons back at Parramatta Stadium a few days later. Typically, it was a milestone which escaped the attention of Soccer Australia, which has never been strong on honouring its players. Typically, Milan Ivanovic didn't go looking for the kudos either. When contacted by a journalist for his reaction to reaching 50 appearances for his adopted country, Ivanovic replied, 'Thank you for remembering.'

Ivanovic, certainly, is a player who deserves to be remembered long after he eventually hangs up his boots. When he arrived in Australia in 1989 from his native Yugoslavia, it was to ostensibly wind down his career. But within two years he was given a new lease of life with the national team, and he never looked back. A player blessed with the innate gift to make time for himself even in the tightest situation, Ivanovic continued to play so well, and so consistently, for the Socceroos that he made it impossible for either Thomson or Venables to drop him.

Indeed, despite playing in a position coveted by two of the country's outstanding talents, Zelic and Okon, the selfless veteran has never suffered in comparison. And he genuinely savoured each and every one of his caps for Australia, which made his 50th appearance especially satisfying. A man not given to displays of emotion, Ivanovic was clearly moved when he ran out onto the pitch at Parramatta against the Solomons that night. Pity there were only empty grandstands to witness the occasion. The official attendance of 2122 was the lowest in history to watch the Socceroos at home in the World Cup.

The Socceroos, with the group all but wrapped up, mirrored the general apathy in a mistake-ridden performance in which even the normally unflappable Ivanovic committed an error or two. The Solomons showed they had learned their lessons well, keeping Australia to a 6–2 scoreline, with three of Australia's goals involving a large element of luck. Apart from a desperately unfortunate own goal, there was a dodgy penalty decision and a comical goal from Slater, his first for his country in his 21st appearance. Slater turned away from a clearance, the ball hit his rear end and ricocheted into the net. 'The arsiest goal ever scored by the Socceroos,' was Arnold's blunt assessment.

The next day, the Socceroos learnt that New Zealand would, as expected, be providing the opposition in the next stage of the campaign. The All Whites had thumped Fiji 5–0 in the decisive match of Group Two, with Rufer again excelling. But nobody in the Australian camp was too concerned. The team was beginning to

TALES FROM OCEANIA

feel it could take on anybody in the world—and win.

Perhaps there was a degree of cockiness. Perhaps the players were distracted by what awaited them in New Zealand. Whatever the case, the Socceroos looked disinterested and disjointed in wrapping up the first stage of the qualifiers with a 2–0 win over Tahiti in their final match. But on a forgettable evening two positives were to emerge: stopper Popovic made his first appearance of the campaign and lasted the full 90 minutes, while Zelic confirmed his growing self-belief with a dominant display crowned by a superbly-struck opening goal.

It may have been a limp performance by the Socceroos, but it was difficult to be harsh. The team had achieved what it had set out to do, and with a minimum of fuss. Four games, four wins. Twenty-six goals for, only two against. Of the 26 players in camp, 25 got on the park. Nobody got injured, and nobody got upset. Next stop Auckland, and hardly a care in the world. Mission accomplished. Part one.

CHAPTER 9

TAMING THE KIWIS

AH, NEW ZEALAND. THE AULD ENEMY. The so-called minnows who lift a notch every time they play Australia. Difficult. Awkward. Historically, a formidable obstacle. But this time Venables and his players were not only well-prepared, they were brimming with confidence, the theory being that times had changed—for the better.

For the All Whites, times had also changed. Since their last meeting with the Socceroos in January, they had changed their coach and many of their players. The gritty Englishman Keith Pritchett had been replaced by Irishman Joe McGrath, originally brought to New Zealand the previous year as director of coaching.

Player power had played a significant role in the changeover; or more particularly, Rufer power. New Zealand's most decorated footballer, Wynton Rufer, had fallen out with Pritchett during a tour to the Middle East some months previously, and although it was never said publicly, those in the know were well aware of the obvious: while Pritchett was in charge, Rufer would never play for the national team.

In the end, the All Whites needed their best player more than they needed their coach. So just before the World Cup qualifiers began, Pritchett made way. His cause had not been helped by the poor results in Australia in January and his conservative selection policies at the expense of youth. The likes of skipper Rodger Gray, Graham Marshall, Andy Rennie and Perry Cotton had all either passed their use-by date or were about to reach the point of no return. The style of player favoured by Pritchett—big and strong but essentially one-dimensional—belonged to a bygone era. Against teams who had speed of both mind and body, they were too often ruthlessly exposed.

Realising that time was running out, and that Rufer was badly needed both on and off the pitch, Soccer New Zealand moved on Pritchett in March. Out went the Englishman, and in came the Irishman who had spent some time working under Jack Charlton during Eire's golden era of the early 1990s.

McGrath's promotion had been 'unofficially' sanctioned in advance by Rufer, who by then was in the throes of winding down his professional club career in the German second division with Kaiserslautern.

When McGrath finally assumed control, there were still more than three months left until the Oceania play-offs. Yet time remained New Zealand's number one enemy. Not even the return of the prodigal son could be guaranteed to turn the sinking ship around. The overwhelming feeling in Auckland was that, Rufer or not, the All Whites would need a miracle to eliminate the Socceroos from the World Cup race.

The enormity of the task became painfully obvious in New Zealand's opening World Cup qualifier on a bumpy pitch in Port Moresby at the end of May. A Rufer-less side was effectively a rudder-less side, and the All Whites succumbed 1–0 to a Papua New Guinea team playing in the competition for the first time. It was the most embarrassing result in New Zealand's World Cup history, and back home fears were raised that the campaign might be over before it had even begun.

Certainly if the All Whites went on to lose their next match in Ba, against the unpredictable Fijians, those fears would be realised. In the event, after a few days spent revitalising their battered morale at the Gold Coast en route to Fiji, a single goal from Chris Jackson restored New Zealand's fortunes. After a 50/50 split on the road, the team headed home confident it now had the ammunition to turn its stuttering campaign around.

The next qualifier against PNG would mark Rufer's eagerly awaited return. The players lifted, visibly, in anticipation. And the no. 7 with the shuffling gait and razor-sharp eye did not disappoint. Officials were caught by surprise as 10 500 fans converged on North Harbour Stadium in Auckland to witness Rufer's first game on home turf for four years. The 34-year-old led the team by example, grabbing a brace of goals—including a stunning free kick bent around the wall—in a critical 7–0 win.

All that now stood between the All Whites and a match-up against the Socceroos was their final group qualifier, against Fiji, to be played on the same ground a week later. And this time just over 13 000 streamed into the stadium on a bitterly cold night to see Rufer again work his magic, scoring another two goals in an encouraging 5–0 win. In a country where the shirt that matters is All Black, suddenly the public began to rally behind the All Whites. Anything seemed possible with the masterful Rufer back in the side. But amid the euphoria, wiser heads sounded a note of caution. The Socceroos, they warned, would be a different proposition altogether.

Australia, for their part, knew what to expect. Three weeks earlier, in the days between the Superstars series and the opening qualifier against the Solomons, Venables and Blanco had flown to Ba to spy on the All Whites. On their return to Sydney, both men were predictably diplomatic. But it was what they didn't say that provided an insight. The inference was that, Rufer aside, the All Whites were unlikely to offer any surprises.

But there was, at the very least, the weight of history to take into account. In six World Cup campaigns dating back to 1973, Australia had won just once in Auckland—in 1993. Twice during that period the All Whites had succeeded in eliminating Australia from the World Cup. In 1981 a bumbling 2–0 loss at the Sydney Cricket Ground cost coach Rudi Gutendorf his job in the hours after the game. Eight years later an over-confident Australian team, having beaten the All Whites 4–1 in Sydney just days before they flew to Auckland, fell to another decisive defeat against a New Zealand team hell-bent on revenge. (The fact that there were just 3000 people at Mt Smart that morning, and the game kicked off at 11 a.m. as a curtain-raiser to an All Black rugby trial, only added insult to the injury.)

As always, in 1997 the All Whites savoured the prospect of putting their trans-Tasman rivals in their place. It was an intensity Venables could well identify with. He had been raised, after all, on the oldest rivalry in world football: Scotland versus England. In most ways, the Antipodean version was tame by comparison, yet the trip to Auckland represented a potential banana-skin all the same.

The key, Venables argued, was to treat the All Whites with the appropriate amount of respect. Rufer was, unquestionably, a world-class footballer even if he was in the twilight of his career. Goalkeeper Jason Batty had impressed with a string of superb performances in Australia in January. The ageless Mike McGarry continued to exhibit sublime close skills, although his best moments came in smaller doses. And up front, the bullocking presence of Darren McClennan had upset the Socceroos' normally unflappable defence on more than one occasion.

Back at the Parramatta Parkroyal in the hours after the final group game against Tahiti, the likes of Arnold, Slater and Aurelio Vidmar had counselled their younger

TAMING THE KIWIS

teammates against taking too much for granted. They knew the dangers of underestimating New Zealand. In one corner Arnold was reminding Moore that the 1989 loss remained the darkest day of his career. Slater, sitting alongside, was making the same point to Muscat. Vidmar was telling his protege, Aloisi, that the All Whites were never more dangerous than when they were backed into a corner. If the forthcoming play-offs appeared to be a formality, they weren't. It was as simple as that.

Others in the bar that night listened to the conversation and admired the leadership shown by the senior players. But how much of it was being taken in? Around the room the talk was not only of the next obstacle in the World Cup campaign, of the matches coming up against New Zealand. There were other topics of conversation, and they loomed as a serious distraction.

The hot topic, it seemed, was transfers. In the hours after the match, and in the days that followed, Bingley was to arrange his move from Marconi-Fairfield to Vissel Kobe in Japan. Zdrilic would finalise his transfer from Sydney United to Grasshoppers Zurich of Switzerland. The presence of Portsmouth manager Terry Fenwick, propped at the bar, was like a magnet to the local players hoping to take their talents overseas. These were the days when Kalac, Enes and Foster would all decide to give Fenwick the next years of their careers. And all the while Venables sat at his table, sharing a bottle of red wine with Blanco and Hill, as the bidding—some of it frantic—went on around him.

Minds on the job, minds on the job. In the wee hours at the nightclub next door, several senior players expressed their concern that the transfer talk was beginning to get out of control. The team had to refocus on the task at hand. That had to be the priority for Venables when he regathered his players at Brighton-le-Sands after giving them the weekend off to spend with their friends and families. Beating the Solomons and Tahiti? Big deal. The Socceroos, in reality, had never been stretched.

It was then that Rufer played a clever hand. If there really was an atmosphere of over-confidence in the Australian camp, he was ready to exploit it. In a newspaper interview over the weekend, Rufer readily predicted that the Socceroos would not only beat his team, but would go on to qualify for the World Cup finals and do well when they got there. 'You've got so many good players, you won't be going [to France] just to make up the numbers,' Rufer said.

Arriving back in camp after a three-day break, the players were told by Venables to forget about what they may have thought, what they may have read, or what they may have been told. The two games against New Zealand represented a fresh start. And there was no margin for error, for there was too much at stake. The Socceroos simply had to win through, and to do that they needed to concentrate. This was for keeps.

For the first time in the campaign, the team went behind closed doors to train at St George Stadium that first afternoon. In the matches against Tahiti and the Solomons, Venables had been relaxed enough, confident enough, to give 25 of his 26 squad players a run. The odd man out, Zdrilic, had been released from the squad over the weekend to join his new club in Switzerland. But as of now, the time for experimenting was over. Away from the prying eyes of the media, Venables began to work with his first-choice XI. Soccer Australia had chosen 'No Second Prize' as its theme song for the World Cup qualifiers. The words began to take on a real meaning.

In the three days before their scheduled departure for Auckland, the Socceroos ironed out the wrinkles. Morale, already high, was fortified when word of an incredible result by the Young Socceroos in Malaysia filtered through. In their final group match at the World Youth Championships, the under-20s had beaten Argentina 4–3. The star of the show was Adelaide City youngster Kosta Salapasidis. He hadn't scored in 49 appearances in the national league, but here he was grabbing all four goals against the world champions. In the breakfast room at the Brighton-le-Sands hotel the following morning, Salapasidis was the name on everyone's lips. Virtually all of the Socceroo players had been through the youth system, and to a man they were inspired by this latest achievement. That afternoon, in their final training session before departure, the Socceroos showed they meant business.

Watched by the media for the first time in a week, the players tore into each other in a training game reminiscent of the 'mad dog' era of Frank Arok. There was a bite in the tackle, a desperation in the play. Whatever hopes they may have had, the players still didn't know for sure if they were in the team. And Venables, smiling benignly, wasn't ready to tell them just yet. Foster and Horvat finished a torrid session with ice packs nursing their bruises. But in the context of hardening the team's resolve, this was a small price to play.

At the same time, across the Tasman, the contrast in preparation couldn't have been more pronounced. McGrath was barely able to scrape up enough players for a six-a-side match as he trained his squad at Auckland's exclusive Kristen School. His skipper, Gray, was a part-time footballer and a full-time detective. On this morning, Gray was required to give evidence in court. The stopper, Hay, missed

Previous page: Alex Tobin runs up the ground with the ball after Australia's first goal against Iran at the Melbourne Cricket Ground. TONY FEDER/SPORTING PIX
Above: Australia's Stan Lazaridis. TONY FEDER/SPORTING PIX

Previous page: Australian socceroo Harry Kewell. CLAYTON/THE SYDNEY MORNING HERALD
Above: Australian socceroo Graham Arnold. SEAN GARNSWORTHY/SPORTING PIX

TAMING THE KIWIS

the session to sit a university exam. And Rufer was excused to appear on a television show. Just three days before the match that would effectively decide their World Cup hopes, the All Whites could only train in bits and pieces. Hardly ideal preparation, as McGrath admitted at a press conference the following day. 'The truth is we don't have a lot of money to offer our players, so what can you do?' he remarked.

Indeed. Here was Venables, with his mega-salary, and a squad which included players earning around $25 000 per week, up against McGrath, on a modest salary by comparison and with just one player—Rufer—who could be regarded as a professional. It had to be a mismatch, didn't it?

Venables was to settle on his starting line-up the night before the team left Sydney, and there were no real surprises. Perhaps the only bone of contention had been whether Arnold would retain his spot ahead of Mori. Arnold got the nod, which meant the Socceroos would go onto the pitch at Albany with nine foreign-based professionals and two locals—Foster and Tobin—both of whom were full-time footballers in the national league.

Match day finally arrived. The Socceroos had been waiting four long years for this. As kick-off approached, traffic leading into the ground was chaotic. By the time the turnstiles clicked over for the last time, more than 23 000 fans had made their way into the ground. On a surprisingly mild winter's evening, it was to be the biggest crowd to watch the All Whites at home since 1981. And the terrace rendition of 'God Defend New Zealand' was suitably evocative in the minutes before Japanese referee Okada Masayoshi at last got the game under way.

In the warm-up, the Australians suffered a late blow when Horvat pulled out, not wanting to risk his injured knee. Ivanovic, as he was to do again months later in Tunisia, stepped smoothly into the breach.

It was a typically frenetic opening. Both sets of players lost their footing on the loose, sandy surface. Lazaridis went down under a scything tackle. Zelic and Jackson began to get a bit testy. The crowd jeered Slater as he slipped while attempting a cross. But a pattern was emerging. The All Whites looked flat in attack and nervous in defence. The Socceroo midfield was getting most of the ball. Rufer was being forced away from the penalty area. And when he did venture into dangerous positions, the reliable Moore was quick to close down his options.

After 19 minutes, the Socceroos broke through. A bad mistake by van Steeden allowed Foster in behind the last line, and Aloisi was on the end of a return pass to finish from close range. The Australian bench erupted. To date, this was the decisive moment of Venables' reign. In the match which mattered most, his team had drawn first blood. From then on, New Zealand played like a beaten side.

A superbly crafted goal from Aurelio Vidmar just before the break confirmed the obvious. As the half-time whistle blew, the crowd fell silent. A sense of inevitability hung in the air. The Socceroos were confident, assured and imaginative. The All Whites were second-rate by comparison. Even the local hero, Rufer, could not arrest the slide.

Goal number three for the Socceroos came late in the match from Foster, capping a dominant, man-of-the-match performance. After having a hand in the first two goals, his shot which ballooned over the keeper was a fitting reward. For too long Foster's career had been blighted by unfulfilled promise. Here, at the age of 28, the gifted midfielder had finally arrived on the big stage.

Pity New Zealand. The final straw came when Jackson was sent off shortly after Foster's goal for a reckless challenge on Zelic. The fans streamed for the exits, the dream having died before their eyes.

An upbeat mood permeated the after-match press conference. Venables spoke glowingly of the professionalism of his players, of their tactical awareness, and of their level of commitment in a testing environment. Surprisingly, McGrath and his skipper, McGarry, were smiling too, warm in their praise of the Socceroos. They readily conceded the obvious, that they had been handsomely beaten by a much better side.

There was, of course, the outstanding matter of the return leg to be played in Sydney in seven days time. But without saying as much, both McGrath and McGarry clearly viewed it as a lost cause. Venables, predictably, was quick to refute suggestions that the contest was over. But if the rubber wasn't dead, it was mortally wounded. Nobody could see the All Whites coming back from here.

The Socceroo players partied hard into the night. Stretch limousines were hired to carry them to bars and nightclubs around the city. Bosnich, as is his habit, opened the wrapping on a big, fat Cuban cigar. The feeling of relief among the players was palpable. Arnold, Trimboli, Tobin, and Slater—the only survivors from the debacle of 1989—had finally exorcised the demons. And weren't they happy about it.

A bleary-eyed squad flew back into Sydney the next day, and were promptly given the day off from training. The newspaper and television coverage was lavish in its praise. Venables reiterated the theme that the job had only been half-done, but nobody was really listening.

TAMING THE KIWIS

Two days later the All Whites flew into town, and the news for them had only got worse. Rufer had pulled out of the return leg, claiming a hamstring strain. He had gone home to Wellington, taking the All Whites' feeble hopes with him.

It was to be a quiet week leading up to the final match of Australia's Oceania campaign. Soccer Australia tried hard to drum up interest, but the edge simply wasn't there. McGrath and Venables were brought together for a press conference at the Sydney Casino, but the rhetoric had a hollow ring. If there was to be a war at the Sydney Football Stadium, it was to be a phoney one; the battle had already been won.

But in the end, the coup de grace was to be delayed. When the players woke up on match day, they looked out to Botany Bay and could barely see the water's edge. It rained, and it just kept on raining. For Soccer Australia, it was to be a dampener in more ways than one. The federation needed a 30 000 crowd to help absorb some of the massive losses it had incurred over the previous month of the campaign. Hill insisted the target would be met, and kept insisting even as the heavens opened up with a vengeance in the hours before the kick-off.

But Mother Nature was in no mood to relent. The water kept tumbling down and the pitch started to resemble a lake. With no sign of a let-up, the sensible decision was taken. The game would be postponed. Police went out to Taylor Square and Cleveland Street to turn motorists away. It was a decision that was to cost Soccer Australia at least $250 000 in desperately needed revenue. But it was the right move all the same. The game was rescheduled for Parramatta Stadium the following night.

The players were frustrated but they were to hold their nerve. Venables had toyed briefly with the idea of dropping Bosnich, who had been less than impressive in Auckland, for Kalac. But in the end he went with the status quo. It was an unchanged Socceroo side that finally took the field at Parramatta against a New Zealand team denied the suspended Jackson and the injured Rufer. McGrath had little choice but to throw in his youngsters. In came Rowe, Stevens and Viljoen, and they did not let themselves down. The All Whites gave a better account of themselves, but it was Australia who again won the game.

A sweet strike by Zelic, clearly rejuvenated by his return to the national team after a dreadful season at club level, gave the Socceroos the lead before half-time. Arnold, playing his best game in the green and gold for many years, completed the job with a clever finish midway through the second half. New Zealand had been eliminated, and with some room to spare.

In the final analysis, it was the pedigree of Australia's squad of European-based professionals that had shone through. The gap between the two nations was now at its widest point. The Socceroos were too polished, too poised, in every respect. The All Whites were left with a lot of thinking to do.

'My feeling is that we were beaten before a ball had been kicked,' reflected a former New Zealand international, Clint Gosling. 'The younger boys were overawed by the reputations of the Australian players. The older guys didn't come up to scratch, and I include Wynton in that. It used to be that a New Zealand team would roll up its sleeves and have a go, but this time they basically gave it away. Not enough bottle. That's what disappointed me the most.'

The Socceroos, by contrast, were on a roll. France 98 was beckoning. Just two games to go.

CHAPTER 10

TENSION BUILDS

WHAT TO DO NEXT? THAT WAS THE THOUGHT uppermost in the minds of both players and coaching staff after the matches against New Zealand had been completed. Nobody wanted to take their eyes off the prize; it was too enticing.

Five long months stretched between the Oceania play-offs and the final, decisive, stage of the World Cup campaign. With the European season almost upon them, players would soon disperse across the globe. Venables, for his part, would spend only a few days relaxing in Sydney before returning to London. The key issue remained: how to maintain the momentum?

It was a momentum that had gathered steam during the Oceania section of the campaign, when the squad had spent its longest spell together under Venables. Relationships had been developed, teamwork had been honed, a bond had been formed. Nobody, least of all the players, wanted to lose sight of the primary objective.

But, of course, there were other pressing matters to consider. For the players, the focus inevitably turned to their club careers, with many Socceroos contemplating a change of scenery. Portsmouth, again, seemed a favoured destination.

For Venables, the business of running his club also became a priority. There was much to organise as Pompey prepared for a season in which promotion to the Premier League was a clear, and much desired, objective. Venables, too, had another round of court appearances to factor into his already tight schedule. So it was that when the coach flew out of Kingsford Smith Airport seven days after the victory at Parramatta Stadium, nothing, in terms of the Socceroos, had been arranged.

Soccer Australia, meantime, had added up its bills from the Oceania campaign and its worst fears were realised. The red ink poured out from underneath its Paddington headquarters. Total losses for the six-week period of the Superstars series and World Cup qualifiers amounted to around $1 million—approximately 18 per cent of the organisation's annual budget. The consolation was that the aim on the park had been achieved, and Hill's confidence remained unshakeable. As long as Australia qualified for the World Cup, he predicted, the investment would yield the appropriate dividend. Until then, it was a matter of lasting the distance.

To accommodate its cash-flow problems, Soccer Australia arranged to extend its overdraft with the National Australia Bank to $950 000. Bills, after all, needed to be paid. The national body had also taken a $250 000 advance from its purse for qualifying for the Confederations Cup to bolster its immediate balance.

Hill had another ace up his sleeve. But until that hand was revealed, Soccer Australia had to sit tight. And as the weeks dragged on, and still there was no sign of another fixture for the national team, the criticism began to mount. The perception mirrored in the daily press was that Soccer Australia simply couldn't afford to get the team together again until the play-offs in Asia. There was basically no money in the bank.

Players, particularly those looking for a way back into the squad, became increasingly agitated. Even those already in favour were disconcerted.

'We've simply got to find the money,' said Arnold, from Japan. 'We will be playing against a team that have just come out of their own qualifying round. They'll be fit, match-hardened and ready. We can't afford to just turn up on the day and hope it works out for the best.'

Back in London, Venables was pestering his contacts to sound out possible opponents for the Socceroos. But the timing was difficult—the European season had begun and the fixture list for August and September was already cluttered with both international and club commitments. The negotiations, as a consequence, were long and involved and the level of frustration grew.

Hill, for his part, was trying to see if the face-to-face discussions he had had earlier in the year during a trip to Europe to see the Macedonia game would yield anything concrete. Austria, Croatia, Greece, Poland—they had all made encouraging noises. But as the weeks marched on, both Hill and Venables continued to draw a blank.

Venables then issued a public challenge for his old employers, England, to host his Australian team at Wembley. Not only would this be a promoter's dream, with

TENSION BUILDS

the former England manager up against his successor, Glenn Hoddle, but it was also a cherished ambition of Australian soccer.

The Socceroos had met England five times at full international level, but never at the spiritual home of football. Yet even with Venables championing the cause, the Football Association refused to commit itself. The same old excuses, sadly, emanated from Lancaster Gate.

And all the time the public clamour to see the Socceroos back in action, at the very least on television, grew. Tired of suggestions that the inactivity was being caused by Soccer Australia's limited resources, Hill hit back. 'Let me make it absolutely clear,' he said. 'Money is not the issue. Terry can have as many games and as many camps as he wants. We are not scrimping on anything. We have told Terry that we will continue to resource our World Cup campaign. The truth is, it's very hard to get games.'

Suddenly, out of left field, came the news that the World Cup holders, Brazil, were prepared to visit Australia to play the Socceroos. A manna from heaven, it seemed. It was a deal cobbled together by private promoters, and supported, allegedly, by Brazil's new major sponsors, Nike. Even a date—early September—had been pencilled in.

Hill listened to the proposal but was not convinced. With the Brazilians insisting on retaining the international television rights alongside their seven-figure match fee, he couldn't see how Soccer Australia could break even, let alone make any money. And his organisation simply couldn't afford another loss-maker, even for Brazil.

A curious sidelight to the deal was that Brazil were also demanding that the Socceroos field their full-strength side, foreign legion et al. The Brazilians even knew the names of the players they wanted to appear in the green and gold—an interesting reversal of roles, if ever there was one. For decades, of course, Australia had been dudded by a succession of touring teams bringing their second-string XIs on tour. But now, with Venables and his players scattered across Europe and unable to return, the boot was on the other foot. 'Socceroos dud the world champions'—now there's a headline!

August ambled on, with Venables and Hill increasingly distracted by other issues. For Hill there was the court action initiated by the Sydney United club, who were embittered by his stance following crowd trouble at the previous season's preliminary final. At the time, Hill had made it clear the Pumas could well be thrown out of the national league if charges of bringing the game into disrepute were proven. Sydney

United took a pre-emptive strike. Former Liberal Party leader John Hewson, now installed as their chairman, took the fight for survival into the New South Wales Supreme Court. The Hewson versus Hill confrontation was about to get personal.

Venables, too, had his attentions diverted from the Socceroos with his club, Portsmouth, looking to build on a solid start to their first-division campaign. The last of his Australians to be signed, Aloisi, was beginning to look the goods. Five goals in his first seven appearances not only helped Pompey, they also aided Aloisi's own World Cup cause. A nice time, and a nice place, to be scoring, that's for sure.

In the meantime, Foster was still waiting for his work permit to come through, while Enes and Kalac had been knocked back by the immigration authorities and Portsmouth were left to consider their next course of action. Club, rather than country, was taking up most of Venables' time.

But finally the breakthrough arrived. In the first week of September, Soccer Australia closed a deal for the Socceroos to play against Tunisia. The North Africans possessed a fine record in international competition, and had already qualified for France '98. The match would be played at the El Menzah Stadium in Tunis on 1 October. Most of the Socceroos had never heard of the place, but they were relieved at the prospect of a few days in camp and a competitive game. It was now evident that this would be the only chance for the team to get together before their World Cup fate was decided. The game, therefore, assumed critical importance; match no. 12 for Venables was to be his biggest test yet.

A few days after the Tunisia match was confirmed came another major announcement. Flanked by the Victorian premier, Jeff Kennett, Hill revealed that Australia's final World Cup qualifier on 29 November would be played at the 100 000 capacity Melbourne Cricket Ground. The ace had fallen out of his sleeve.

Two more conventional soccer venues, the Sydney Football Stadium and Lang Park in Brisbane, were to be overlooked. The reasoning was simple. Victoria, and in particular its Major Events Corporation, had made Hill an offer that was too good to refuse. Soccer Australia would receive income equivalent to a gate of 62 000 people. After taking out expenses, Hill made a quick calculation that at least $2 million would be guaranteed before a ball was kicked. As a sweetener, the Victorians also threw in an advance of $250 000. In the circumstances, it was no surprise that Hill grabbed the offer. The dollars made sense.

So now there was a time and a place confirmed for Australia's biggest match since the famous 1993 qualifier against Argentina, which was played at the same stage of the World Cup campaign. That match at the SFS had been a sell-out, and

T/E/N/S/I/O/N B/U/I/L/D/S

Hill confidently predicted the same response at the MCG. One hundred thousand at a soccer match in Australia? Hill wanted to see that.

All Venables wanted to see, as a priority, was his players. The gathering point was to be the appropriately named El Mechtel Hotel in Tunis. The date: 28 September. And there was one player who Venables wanted on board above all—his wayward striker, Viduka. Selection-wise, it was to be the toughest call of his Socceroo reign so far. Practically, it was also to prove a hard choice to fulfil.

In the months since he had controversially opted out of his call-up for the Oceania qualifiers, Viduka may have been out of sight but he had not been out of mind. Croatia Zagreb were set to play two high-profile opponents in the European Champions League, and Viduka's name was bound to figure prominently in proceedings.

In the qualifying round, Zagreb had been pulled out of the hat with, of all teams, Partizan Belgrade. Politically and emotionally, it was a nightmare come true—a Croatian team against a Serbian team for the first time since the end of the holocaust that was the Yugoslav war. Tensions in the region remained high, with memories of the atrocities committed by both sides still fresh in people's minds.

And if the Croatians got past their near neighbours, then waiting in the wings in the first round would be one of England's glamour sides, Newcastle United; this at a time when Viduka was being linked to a big-money transfer to England, with Manchester United and Arsenal leading the bidding. He was being given the chance to strut his $11 million pedigree on the perfect stage.

It is history that Viduka and his teammates ultimately, and convincingly, triumphed over two legs in their powder-keg meeting with their Balkan rivals. And so it was on to St James Park, in the north-east of England, where Viduka, in his club strip, and Venables, there in his television role with ITV, were finally to come face-to-face.

It was a chance meeting, the significance of which was totally lost on those inside the ground. Viduka broke away from the warm-up to run across to the sideline, where Venables was presenting for ITV. Amid the din of the Newcastle crowd, a brief discussion ensued, the thrust of which Venables was later to recall.

'Basically he told me he would never, ever, not want to play for his country,' Venables said. 'We intended to have a proper discussion after the game, but Mark's team got a very bad decision and the players went straight to the bus and left. Clearly, though, Mark believes what happened in June wasn't his fault.'

With the ice broken, others were trying to mend the bridges. The International

Management Group (IMG) was in the throes of trying to tie Viduka to a long-term contract, and the company believed a flourishing Socceroo career was a crucial factor in his marketability. One of IMG's Australian-based representatives, Bernie Mandic, contacted Venables to reinforce the basis of the brief chat that had occurred a few days before in Newcastle. Mandic emphasised to the coach that his client was truly genuine in wanting to play for Australia.

A few weeks later, Venables announced a 24-man squad for the Tunisia game. Viduka's name was on the list.

If it was the recall of Viduka that dominated the headlines (and was to provide another unexpected twist), there were two other interesting decisions made by Venables and his assistant, Blanco, for the Tunisia game.

Paul Okon was continuing on a slow and painful road to recovery after his well-publicised groin and knee problems, and was included in the squad in the hope he could mark his green and gold comeback in Tunis. Australia's best player had yet to play for Venables, and his return was eagerly anticipated. Sadly, it was not to be. The Lazio utility lost this particular battle for fitness.

But Okon, at least, was reassured that he was in Venables' plans. The same could not be said for Arnold, at that point a veteran of 54 internationals for Australia, the last of which—the return leg of the Oceania play-offs against New Zealand—had been one of his best. Incredibly, Arnold was left out of the squad, creating the obvious conclusion that with Viduka back in, he was out. Those who had expected the Arnold/Viduka combination to lead Australia's attack in November were dumbfounded.

Arnold was equally surprised. He'd had no inkling the axe was about to fall, and only found out through a journalist that he had not been selected. There was no phone call from either Venables or Blanco. Understandably, but privately, Arnold fumed.

The official reason given for his absence was that he had not been fit when selection decisions needed to be made. But at the time the squad was announced Arnold had just completed his fifth match in a row for his Japanese club, Sanfrecce, scoring three goals in the process. Clearly, wires had been crossed. Or had they?

Venables maintained that he had omitted Arnold on the advice of Blanco, who had in turn been told by Arnold's club coach, Thomson, that the player had been sidelined with an Achilles problem. True enough, Arnold had missed three weeks in the J League in order to allow his injury to recover from the rigours of World Cup duty. To answer the call of his country, Arnold had played against New Zealand

TENSION BUILDS

with the aid of a cortisone injection. Now he wanted to give his damaged heel time to recover so he could be ready to play against Tunisia.

But he was never to get the chance. At the last moment, when the squad was hit by a spate of late withdrawals, Arnold was indeed asked to join the squad in Tunis. But when the fax arrived at his unit in Hiroshima late on the Friday night, there were only five days left before the match. With the weekend upon him and with no hope of applying for a re-entry visa until the Monday, it was simply impossible for Arnold to get to Tunisia in time. He left a message on Venables' answer-phone, and could only wait and hope it was not the end.

Arnold's replacement, Viduka, did make it to Tunis, but not without a fight. Twenty-four hours before the game, his club was involved in a decisive UEFA Cup game in Switzerland. Having been dumped from the Champions League by Newcastle, the UEFA Cup represented only a consolation prize for Zagreb. But the competition still figured highly in the club's list of priorities for the season, and Viduka was left in no doubt that he would be a required asset in Zurich.

Here we go again, thought Venables. Again there were phone conversations between player and coach. Again Viduka emphasised his desire to play for the Socceroos. Again Soccer Australia went through the formal channels to try to extract Viduka from Zagreb's grasp. And again the club played a high-stakes game of brinkmanship, ignoring the faxes and continuing to heap pressure on Viduka to ignore the call of his country.

It was, Viduka later confided to friend, the hardest decision of his life. If he failed to arrive in Tunis, he could almost certainly forget about playing in the World Cup. And if he did go, there was the risk of severely damaging the relationship with his club which, after all, paid him around $1 million per year.

As Viduka dithered, Venables took matters into his own hands. He telephoned the Zagreb secretary just three days before the deadline and made it clear he would take the club to the highest authority if Viduka was not released. The club, reluctantly, backed down. Viduka could go.

It was the first time Venables had personally intervened on behalf of a player—a show of faith, certainly, in Viduka's talents. Against better class opposition than that provided by Oceania, and with the decisive stage of the World Cup campaign looming, the clear implication was that if Australia wanted to progress, then Viduka needed to be in the team.

But Viduka's enforced departure for Tunis did not come without a cost. On the day of the game, the *Daily Express* in London revealed Venables had received death threats from anonymous Croatians angry about his actions in forcing Viduka's release, and seething over his criticism of the club's behaviour.

'You are dead. We are going to kill you... and we're not joking.' That was the message on his mobile phone. Venables later declined to elaborate on the threats. But his phone was taken by police for the days surrounding the Tunisia game, just in case there were further threats.

Venables flew into Tunis four days before the game. The city was bathed in a heatwave. His assistants, Blanco and Scheinflug, were to join him, having completed spying missions to Japan, Qatar and Dubai on the way over. The dossiers were being updated in preparation for the World Cup play-offs eight weeks down the track.

The dossier on Tunisia, Australia's immediate opponents, was not so well-endowed. Apart from two players employed by Swiss second-division club Fribourg, the Tunisian squad was drawn from inside its own domestic league. Information was scarce.

But Venables knew the North Africans and their Polish coach, Henryk Kasperczak, deserved respect. A few months earlier at the same stadium, they had celebrated their qualification for the World Cup at the expense of their arch rivals, Egypt. Venables, by his own estimation, was taking a chance in agreeing to the fixture. A difficult opponent in difficult conditions. A heavy defeat could have eroded the morale so carefully built up during the Oceania qualifiers.

The build-up didn't go exactly to plan. Having already given his first-choice goalkeeper, Mark Bosnich, the night off to allow him to play for Aston Villa in an important UEFA Cup game, Venables then lost Okon, Lazaridis and Moore to injury in quick succession. Exciting teenager Harry Kewell, earning rave reviews playing for Leeds United under Venables' old mate George Graham, was drafted in to strengthen a depleted squad.

As the players drifted in from their various locations, Venables—to his delight—discovered that the spirit and enthusiasm had not evaporated in the months since the squad had last been together in Sydney. Once again he found the camaraderie, and the keeness, invigorating.

The upbeat mood carried into the game. On a hot, cloying evening, things started off badly. During the warm-up, sweeper Steve Horvat strained a hamstring in a four-a-side game and cried off. Ivanovic, kicking a ball around with the subs on the other side of the pitch, was thrust into action just minutes before the kick-off. And as had been the case in identical circumstances in Auckland three months

T/E/N/S/I/O/N B/U/I/L/D/S

earlier, Ivanovic went on to have a superb game. 'Every time he comes into camp, he says he's here for the last time,' said Aurelio Vidmar. 'But there's no way he can be dropped. The guy's an absolute legend.'

It was Vidmar who got the Socceroos, wearing black shorts and socks for the first time, off to the perfect start. Putting his troubles at club level behind him, Vidmar climbed well for a corner taken by Skoko on the right, and guided his header into the roof of the net. It was 1–0 Australia, and barely a minute into the match.

Shell-shocked, the Tunisians retreated under the Socceroo onslaught. At the back, Ivanovic, Tobin and Tony Vidmar were tight as a drum, even if goalkeeper Kalac was having some shaky moments behind them. In the middle of the park, Zelic and Skoko were busy and inventive, while Aurelio Vidmar continued to threaten down the left. Indeed, it was from a typically damaging burst by Vidmar that Viduka was able to celebrate his recall with a goal, beating the offside trap to latch on to a pass before cleverly chipping the advancing goalkeeper. With Croatia Zagreb having won 5–0 in Switzerland the night before, Viduka's choice of country over club looked to be inspired.

The crowd, suitably impressed, began to cheer the visitors and jeer their own team. The home side responded with their best spell either side of the break, but good chances went begging while Kalac redeemed himself with one fine save down low to deny Sami. Substitute Bingley then wrapped up the match with a third goal towards the end, after the Tunisian goalkeeper Boubaker had failed to hold a rasping drive from another Australian reserve, Kewell.

The chant of 'ole, ole, ole' rained down from the terraces as the Socceroos stroked the ball around, and the players raised their arms in triumph at the final whistle. Twelve wins out of 12 for Venables was reason enough to celebrate, but this was the most impressive result to date.

Seven changes had been made to the starting XI since the previous match against New Zealand, there had been a spate of late withdrawals, and the Socceroos had won 3–0 away from home against a team ranked 16 places higher than themselves on the FIFA rankings. A reason to rejoice, which is exactly what Slater was doing in the hotel bar later that night.

'This would have to be our best performance since Terry took over,' Slater said. 'But let's not get carried away. The important games are still to come.'

CHAPTER 11

THE BIG ONE

IF THE TASK AHEAD OF THE SOCCEROOS remained clearly defined, the identity of their opponents for the World Cup play-offs was anything but. Venables knew the opposition would come from Asia, and he knew it would emerge from the 10 teams involved in the final stages of the regional qualifiers. But that is about all he, or anybody else, knew in the tense, suspenseful weeks leading up to the two-match play-off in late November. It was far from an ideal situation.

Not that the Socceroos, or the nation, lacked in confidence. The win in Tunisia had given the team an enviable record: 12 games under Venables, for 12 wins. Add the two-legged Oceania Nations Cup final against Tahiti played under caretaker coach Blanco, and the last few results achieved by outgoing Eddie Thomson in South Africa and Saudi Arabia, and the Socceroos would be going into the play-offs unbeaten in 16 games played over more than a year. The achievement of 14 consecutive wins, it was later discovered, had broken the old world record set by Scotland almost 100 years earlier. Never had the national team looked in better shape. Never had the wins come so easily and so emphatically. Never had the Socceroos looked so assured of qualifying for the World Cup finals. Everything looked to be in place.

Not that there weren't some distractions. Again Venables found himself in the headlines for the wrong reasons, this time on the receiving end of a less-than-complimentary character reference from a London judge. Justice Timothy Pontius accused the Socceroo coach of misleading the jury in the case involving his long-time business associate Eddie Ashby, who had most recently been employed by Portsmouth in an 'advisory' role. Ashby was jailed for four months for helping Venables run his various businesses, including Scribes, while he was a declared bankrupt.

As usual, Venables took the allegations in his stride. It was not the first time the British establishment he so despised had treated him harshly. And it wouldn't be the last. But if Venables' track record as a businessman continued to leave something to be desired, his status as a coach remained as credible as ever. Despite his impending duties with the Socceroos, various European clubs—among them Benfica (Portugal) and Deportivo la Coruna (Spain)—were already sounding him out about future employment. In his weekly *News of the World* column, Venables admitted Benfica's $2.2 million offer had been very appealing, but added he would not consider breaking his contract with Soccer Australia. 'The World Cup comes first and it's what I'm concentrating on,' he wrote.

As the moment of truth neared, he needed his powers of concentration more than ever. The size and composition of the squad for the play-offs remained the subject of intense speculation, for some important players had been absent from the successful sojourn in Tunis. The injury-plagued Paul Okon and veteran striker Graham Arnold headed the list of those on the outside hoping to get back in. Arnold's absence had come about in puzzling circumstances and the player remained unsure of where he stood, while Okon, who had begun his latest comeback attempt shortly after the Tunisia match, remained equally keen to report for World Cup duty under Venables for the first time. Ditto two of his former Marconi-Fairfield teammates, Steve Corica and Mark Schwarzer, who were both returning from injury. Venables, certainly, had no shortage of talent at his disposal. He was positively spoiled for choice.

In the end, Venables was required to select his squad before he knew the opposition. It was, he said at the time, 'the most confusing situation I have had to deal with in my career'. It was equally confusing for everyone else.

What had seemed to be a relatively straightforward scenario at the time the draw was constructed—the Oceania group winners would meet the fourth-best Asian team for the 32nd and final vacancy in the World Cup—had instead developed into a logistical nightmare. Initially, it had been intended that the winners of the 10 Asian groups would be brought together for one tournament to be played at a neutral venue. Bahrain and Kuala Lumpur were vying for the hosting rights. But the 10 second round qualifiers could not agree among themselves. The wrangling went on for weeks, and neither the world body, FIFA, or the regional body, the Asian Football Confederation (AFC), was prepared to force the issue. Finally, the decision was made to make no decision. There would be no tournament, and instead the teams would be divided into two groups and they would play each other on a home-and-away basis. What was supposed to have been decided within a month—who would earn Asia's three automatic qualifying berths in France 98 and who would meet Australia for the remaining vacancy—would end up taking twice as long to resolve. As a consequence, the Socceroos wouldn't discover who they were playing until just six days before the first game was scheduled. It was a long way from ideal, and Venables knew it.

He also knew he could not delay finalising his squad in the meantime. And what he decided was to retain the policy which had served him well during the Oceania section of the campaign: a big squad with plenty of cover for every position. For financial reasons, Soccer Australia would have preferred a list of 20 players or less. But Hill continued to push the party line—whatever Venables wanted, he would get. There would be no cost-cutting, no short cuts. Again a big squad would be maintained.

When the squad was announced via a video link-up to the Channel Nine studios in Melbourne (Venables was being paid a retainer by the network), 26 names were on the list that counted. Arnold and Okon were included, as was exciting young striker Harry Kewell, who had impressed as a substitute in Tunisia. The notable absentees were Corica and Schwarzer, for differing reasons. Corica, tragically, re-injured his damaged knee the weekend before the squad was finalised. Instead of contemplating World Cup glory, he could only curse his wretched luck.

Schwarzer was equally dispirited. Back in top form for Middlesbrough, he had every right to feel confident of making the squad. Others felt the same way, especially as the third-choice goalkeeper, Jason Petkovic, had hardly been distinguishing himself playing for Adelaide City in the domestic competition. Schwarzer wasn't happy at all, and let it be known. In a scathing outburst, he accused Venables of favouring players from Portsmouth, in particular his goalkeeping rival Zeljko Kalac. At that point Kalac was still seeking a work permit to join Portsmouth. 'There's a pact there and they're pushing Zeljko to be in the team to get him qualified to play overseas and that's the way it is,' said Schwarzer. 'It seems to be a thing for the boys these days.'

Kalac, not surprisingly, was shocked and hurt by the outburst from his childhood friend. 'I am surprised—we're supposed to be mates. It wasn't any other keepers, just me. He's obviously very disappointed, and you don't blame him for that, but I don't expect him to take it out on his peers. You just don't do that.'

Yet if Schwarzer had made a serious tactical error in focusing on Kalac, who by most estimations not only deserved to be in the squad but would be a serious threat to the no. 1 jersey held by Mark Bosnich, his frustration was understandable. In the previous World Cup campaign he had performed heroics in the play-off series against Canada. When Bosnich announced his 'retirement' from the team as a protest at being forced to play in the first leg in Canada, Schwarzer was hurriedly summoned to Edmonton from Sydney as back-up for first choice Robert Zabica. Within 20 minutes he was suddenly thrust into the fray when Zabica was sent off, and he performed with distinction on his senior debut. He held his spot for the return leg in Sydney, and made two brilliant saves in the penalty shoot-out to push the Socceroos through to the final stage against Argentina. Yet Schwarzer was not rewarded for his commitment; far from it. Bosnich suddenly annnounced he was no longer retired, and the hero against Canada was unceremoniously dumped for the games against Diego Maradona and the Argentines. It hurt, but he kept his own counsel. Schwarzer subsequently transferred to Germany, and after three seasons of honing his talents as second choice in the Bundesliga he eventually hit the big time in England. Yet despite his eye-catching form for Middlesbrough, he continued to be overlooked.

Ultimately, it all became too much. When he was omitted from the World Cup squad by Venables, years of frustration welled up and poured into print. His manager at the Riverside Stadium, Bryan Robson, lent his considerable weight to the argument. Ironically, Robson had been on the England coaching staff during Venables' time in charge. Both Robson and Boro's goalkeeping coach, the legendary Peter Shilton, proclaimed their astonishment that Schwarzer had been overlooked. Perhaps, Robson mused, he was paying the price for putting club before country. When the Socceroos had played in Macedonia six months earlier, it had clashed with one of Boro's most important fixtures of the season, the League Cup semifinal against Stockport County.

> 'Australia must have some fantastic goalkeepers if Mark is not selected,' said Robson. 'I worked with Terry in the England set-up and I know that he is a fair minded guy, but I feel he is being unfair to Mark. I would not like to think Terry is holding it against Mark for missing a friendly international. Terry has a great record as a manager, and I am not trying to select his team.

I am simply putting forward the case of someone I class as an outstanding player.'

But to no avail. Schwarzer remained out in the cold.

Venables declined to buy into the debate, despite the obvious temptation. Having finalised his squad, his focus was now on the identity of the opposition. And as October gave way to November, a clearer picture finally began to emerge. South Korea, who had been beaten by the Socceroos in Brisbane early in the year, became the first Asian team to qualify for France 98 after thrashing Uzbekistan 5–1 away. It was left to Japan and the United Arab Emirates to fight out the runners-up position in the group, with the UAE favoured after forcing a scoreless draw in Tokyo. But Japan, with a change of coach, flew to Seoul to play the already qualified Koreans, and miraculously emerged with a 2–0 win. The following week they confirmed their amazing comeback by humbling visiting Kazakhstan 5–1— eliminating the UAE from contention. Japan had now assured themselves of a second chance, but who they would meet in the play-off for Asia's third automatic qualifying spot remained uncertain. In the other group Iran had long looked certain of going directly to France, but suddenly they hit the wall. An agonising loss away to Saudi Arabia, a draw at home against Kuwait, and then a shock 2–0 loss in Qatar threw the group wide open.

Everything now hinged on the group's final qualifying match to be played in Doha, where Qatar would host Saudi Arabia. Three outcomes hinged on the one match. A Qatari win would put the team that had been at the bottom of the group only three weeks earlier through to France 98. A Saudi win would give them a place in the finals for the second time in a row. And a draw would suit Iran, who were watching anxiously from the other side of the Persian Gulf. In the end a single goal settled the issue, and it was the Saudis who were left to rejoice. Qatar were out, and Iran dropped down to the runners-up spot. Across the Indian Ocean, Australia viewed events with increasing anxiety. The spectre of Iran, the one team the Socceroos had been desperate to avoid, began to loom larger.

Iran now had to fly to Johor Bahru, on the southern tip of the Malaysian peninsula, to meet Japan in the final Asian zone play-off. For the winners, the prize was Asia's third automatic place in the World Cup finals. For the losers, Australia were waiting expectantly.

Thousands of viewers woke in the early hours to watch the grainy pictures from Malaysia. Every kick of the ball created different possibilities. The match switched

THE BIG ONE

from end to end. The penalty area was like a pinball machine. It became clearer by the minute that Iran were in truly awful form, yet Japan couldn't put them away. The score 1–0 to Japan became 1–1 just before half-time. Then Ali Daei headed home for Iran. Tokyo, Tehran, Tokyo, Tehran, Tokyo—for the Socceroos, the destination changed by the minute. The match ebbed and flowed. Substitute Shoji Jo knocked in the equaliser for the totally dominant Japanese. They moved in for the kill. Now it would be Tehran, surely. And surely it was. Twenty-five minutes into extra time, another substitute, Masayuki Okano, finally put Iran out of their misery. It was the most golden of goals. The thousands of Japanese fans jumped for joy on a steamy tropical night. After the agonising near-miss the previous campaign, when they had lost out in the final minutes, Japan had finally qualified for their first World Cup. And given that they would be jointly hosting the next one in 2002, it was well timed indeed. The whole football world seemed happy with the outcome—except, of course, Iran and Australia. It left the Socceroos with the trip, and the task, they had been dreading. They had to beat Iran. And they had just six days to prepare.

Iran, it needs to be said, had problems of their own. The fatigue caused by months of trooping around Asia had taken its toll. The players, too, had become exasperated with the coaching style of Mohammed Kohan. After a mutiny led by star players Ahmadreza Abedzadeh, Ali Daei, Khodadad Azizi and midfielder Karim Bagheri, and the loss of Qatar, the coach lost his job. A Brazilian journeyman, Valdier Vierra, who had only just arrived in Tehran to take charge of the Olympic (under-23) team, was suddenly thrust into the role of coaching the senior team. He was appointed two days before Iran left for the play-off against Japan.

The performance in Johor Bahru perhaps reflected the situation. Vierra did not speak the dominant language, Farsi, and he did not know his players by sight or by name. Little wonder the team had looked confused. And now Vierra faced the daunting challenge of lifting the players' battered morale in time to meet the Socceroos over two sudden-death matches—knowing how high the cost of failure would be.

The cost of failure, of course, was high all round. Even though Iran had been the team the Socceroos were desperately hoping to avoid, they remained beatable all the same. Officially, Iran were ranked 49th in the world at the time of the play-offs—16 slots below Australia. In reality, too, the Socceroos had never been handed an easier qualifying route. While Iran deserved respect, they did not rank with the likes of Argentina, Colombia and Scotland—nations that had barred the way during the three previous campaigns. Certainly it was not going to be easy, but in the context of history Australia had never had a better opportunity.

Only the players, however, were honest enough to accept the point. Everyone else seemed intent on hosing down the expectations in case something went wrong.

When Hill chose to call a press conference a few hours after the home-based players flew out of Sydney, the temperature went through the roof. Incredibly, just days before the Socceroos were due to face their biggest match in four years, the chairman succeeded in angering and upsetting the Iranians over a series of comments about the instability of the region, about fears of hygiene, and about a hostile crowd reception. 'Even contamination in the water is enough to potentially knock out your team,' he told reporters in Sydney. The story was in Tehran within hours and created a major diplomatic furore. Not surprisingly, the Iranians were deeply offended, and remain so to this day. Not surprisingly, the Australian players were equally dismayed. As if the job before them wasn't hard enough already. Hill would later back down from some of his statements, and accuse the media of causing mischief. 'In our country we call it a beat-up,' he said. Not only was this disclaimer incorrect, it was also irrelevant—the damage had been done.

As the story was ricocheting its way around the international wire services, the players were flying towards the Middle East from two different directions. From Australia and Japan came the home-based players plus Graham Arnold and Matthew Bingley. From Europe, came the rest. It was in the early hours of the morning, Singapore time, that the Socceroos got their first look at their opponents. The rendezvous occurred in gate lounge C11 of Changi International Airport. The destination was Dubai, on Emirates Air. It was the day after Iran had lost to Japan. A few hours earlier, the Japanese players had passed through the terminal on their way home to Tokyo, mobbed all the way by their adoring fans. Awhile after the commotion subsided, Bingley, Arnold and the home-based Socceroos made their way towards the gate. And there, already waiting, were the Iranians—obviously tired, a little dishevelled, but still full of good spirit and humour. Out in the corridor, Vierra and his assistants were analysing the events of the night before. There was an uncomfortable silence once the realisation dawned upon the two groups of players that, in a delicious coincidence, they would be sharing the same plane over the next seven and a half hours. The psychological battle had begun. But in every respect, there was still a long way to go.

Dubai, the boom city of the Middle East, spread along a sweeping curve of the

THE BIG ONE

Persian Gulf near the tip of the Arabian peninsula that belongs to Oman. Oil-rich. Asset-rich. Rich, rich, rich. Money dripping from every minaret. It was here that Venables had decided to house the Socceroos in the days leading up to the match in Tehran. Assistant coach Les Scheinflug had visited Tehran the previous week and advised against the team spending any longer than necessary in the capital of Iran. It was better, according to Scheinflug, that the Socceroos enjoy the first-class hotels, the First World training facilities, and the new world ambience of Dubai rather than the Third World grime of post-revolutionary Tehran. Venables was happy to agree. And, perchance, he knew the manager of Dubai's newest and most extravagant hotel, the Jumeirah Beach Resort, which was not due to open for a couple more weeks. No matter, the Socceroos would be permitted to stay in what surely must be the most opulent accommodation available anywhere in the world: 600 rooms, 18 restaurants, numerous bars, three swimming pools, a private beach and marina, three squash courts, seven tennis courts, a nine-hole putting green… all housed in a giant, curved complex resembling a tidal wave emerging from the nearby sea. And all this available for a standard rate of $450 per night, or $1600 if you prefer the suite. But for Venables and the boys?—a knockdown price of $150. The Irish manager, Gerald Lawless, was a mate, after all.

The contrast could hardly have been more pronounced. While the Iranian players flew on to Tehran to stay at their own homes and drive their own cars to training, the Socceroos were being treated like rock stars. Rod Stewart, coincidentally, was also sharing their swank seven-star hotel. Goalkeeping coach Ron Corry, a veteran of the 1960s campaigns when the only stars the players saw were the ones high above the rooftop, could only shake his head in wonderment. The Hill mantra echoed around the parquetry corridors, so new they still reeked of varnish; no expense would be spared in the quest to qualify. And it wasn't. Twenty-six players, four coaches, four officials, two physios, one doctor and a gear steward formed the Australian delegation. The only problem was, the players had to keep reminding themselves they were not on an all-expenses-paid holiday. It was purely business.

The business was conducted on the perfectly manicured training pitches of the Al Shabab Club, about 20 minutes drive from the centre of town. While the national league in the United Arab Emirates remains amateur, the facilities are superbly professional. Again, the Socceroos lacked for nothing. Milan Ivanovic even got to catch up with an old friend. The Al Shabab coach was a former teammate at the Yugoslav club Red Star Belgrade. But in a convivial atmosphere, all was not going according to plan. The first day's training was little more than a gentle stroll and a short game because the players had had so little time to get over their jet lag. And in a situation where time was severly constrained, Venables bemoaned the lack of proper preparation. The coach's mood was not helped, either, by two distractions he could have done without. Hill's comments continued to generate headlines, with the Iranian agency IRNA claiming they had been 'malicious, irresponsible and ridiculous'. Hill refused to apologise, all the same. And of perhaps more importance to the coach was a rumour that four key Iranian players whom he had assumed to be suspended—Mohammed Khakpour, Akbar Ostad Asadli, Ahmadreza Abedzadeh and Khodadad Azizi—might be let off the hook. Interestingly, just as FIFA was contemplating its decision, President Joao Havelange was in Tehran as guest of honour at the West Asian Games. A day after Havelange flew out of Iran, the ruling was announced from FIFA headquarters in Zurich. After heavy lobbying from the Asian Football Confederation, of which Iran is a prominent member, an amnesty was declared. On the questionable grounds that the play-off series constituted a separate tournament to the early phase of World Cup qualifiers, the slate would be wiped clean.

Not surprisingly, Venables was livid. 'You may as well say that you can abuse the ref, kick people and get a card because it will be wiped off,' he said. Suddenly, the Iranians looked a much stronger team. But if there was some consolation, it was that key midfielder Karim Bagheri had not escaped an earlier two-match suspension which followed his sending off in Qatar. Bagheri would miss the game in Tehran.

So, too, would Paul Okon. The Socceroos' outstanding player turned up in Dubai complaining of stiffness in his damaged knee, and on the advice of the medical staff was not considered for selection. It was a savage blow for the player, who was still waiting to play under Venables for the first time, and a major blow to the team. Venables had flown to Rome to watch Okon play in a reserve team game for Lazio three weeks earlier, and was cautiously optimistic he would meet the deadline. A fit and focused Okon would have been a a big plus for the team, but it was not to be. Venables was instead left to consider the claims of Ivanovic and Steve Horvat for the crucial sweeper's role.

There was another injury problem, as well. Stan Lazaridis had missed the previous six weeks for his English club, West Ham, with a groin strain, and arrived in Dubai underdone. He worked separately with physio Bill Collins, but time was always going to be against him. Ultimately, Lazaridis was not to be risked, and was left to start the match on the bench.

Aside from the usual selection/injury issues, Venables and his players were left

THE BIG ONE

to prepare in peace. In a practice unknown in all previous campaigns, the Australian media was banned from staying in the same hotel, banned from talking casually to players, and banned from gaining interviews except at times approved by Venables. In a fortnight when the profile of the game was set to reach an all-time high, Soccer Australia chose to treat the media with disdain. Hill continued to insist that his comments about Iran had been taken out of context by the press, while on occasions the players were physically shepherded away from journalists—some of whom they had known as friends for 15 years.

One story, however, refused to die. Insulted by Hill's outburst, the Iranian mood darkened further when it was learnt that the Socceroos would be taking their own chef to Tehran, and were trying to arrange a special flight out of the city just a few hours after the end of the game. A Maltese cook was seconded from the Jumeirah Beach Hotel, and flown to Tehran with team manager Charlie Caruso 24 hours before the players. And after an earlier plan to divert a regular Qantas commercial flight to Tehran foundered, Soccer Australia finally succeeded in organising a charter flight to fly from Tehran to Dubai straight after the match. The contingent of Australian media asked Hill if they might occupy the spare seats, but were brusquely turned away.

And so it was on to the capital of Iran. Spread underneath the slopes of the Elburz Mountains, Tehran boasts an impressive backdrop of snowy peaks. If only they were visible. The sprawling city of 12 million people seems to be in danger of choking in its own pollution, most of it caused by millions of banged-up cars spewing thick, black plumes of diesel into the air. Old-time residents fondly recall the Tehran of 30 years earlier, when the air was clean, the mountains were green, and the trip over Mt Damavand for a holiday on the Caspian Sea took an hour. Nowadays, it takes half a day.

The Socceroos arrived the day before the game in a city that appeared to seize up under the strain of its crumbling infrastructure. But if the population was largely impoverished, the prevailing mood was that life was starting to look up again. A country that had enthusiastically embraced westernisation under the Shah had been brought back to earth by the Islamic revolution and the subsequent bloody war with Iraq. Yet the people remained resilient, and the government was showing signs of moderation. The feeling of a nation that had known the worst of times was that better times were just around the corner. Success against the Socceroos would help to restore morale.

The propaganda battle intensified on the eve of the match. The Farsi-language *Iran Daily* opined: 'Iran is a proud and honourable nation. Its fans are anything but rough and rowdy… the irresponsible statements by the Australian officials have turned this match into a war as Iranian fans won't tolerate these comments and will respond appropriately during the upcoming game. It is also interesting to note that the Australian Embassy in Tehran has not distanced itself from these malicious remarks but, by its ongoing silence, has actually condoned them. But then again, one shouldn't accept [sic] too much from a nation that started out as a former prison camp of the British.'

The players didn't know whether to laugh or cry. The normally jovial Australian first secretary, Peter McCready, who had been an enormous help to the press, was less than amused.

Given the mood outside, it was not surprising that the players were content to remain inside their hotel for most of the 36 hours before kick-off. The Esteghlal Grand—the Hilton in pre-revolutionary days—reeked of faded grandeur. But the food was good and the staff were friendly. There were customs to be observed nonetheless. Twice, goalkeeper Mark Bosnich came down to the lobby in a pair of shorts, and both times he was ordered back to his room to put on tracksuit pants.

Bosnich and the other players were permitted to show their bare legs, however, when they ventured to the match venue, the Azadi Stadium, for a light training run on the evening before the game. A few hundred curious spectators had remained behind from the earlier Iranian session, and the players were greeted with the predictable chorus of 'Iran, Iran' when they arrived at the ground. They were disillusioned by what they saw. A bumpy, uneven pitch with several bare patches around one of the penalty areas was as bad as they had feared. Ball control was going to be a lottery.

Match day dawned, and it was a special day for one player in particular. Robbie Slater, a veteran of two previous campaigns, hoped to celebrate his 33rd birthday with a result that would make it a case of third time lucky. For a player who had spent the best years of his career in France, qualifying was especially important. Venables had announced his team the previous afternoon, and the only real point of contention—whether Ivanovic or Horvat would play sweeper—went the way of the latter. Harry Kewell, just 19 years old but blessed with the arrogance of youth, would be starting alongside Viduka in attack.

By 9 a.m., still six hours before kick-off, an estimated 40 000 people were already inside the ground. With an entry price of 500 rials (about $1), football remains an

THE BIG ONE

affordable, and approved, diversion for a population starved of entertainment. But that only applies to the men. Women are banned from attending male sports events; they can only watch other women play sport. It didn't affect the attendance at all. This was the most important match played in Iran for 20 years, when they had last met Australia on their way to qualifying for the 1978 finals in Argentina. The Azadi Stadium held 128 000 fans, and there wasn't a spare seat in the house.

There wasn't much room outside, either. The freeways were jammed with cars, trucks and buses, and the Socceroos almost didn't make it through. The plan had been for a convoy, which included a bus for the media, to be guided to the stadium by police escort. But when the bus designated for the media failed to arrive, pandemonium erupted. Journalists and cameramen commandeered any available transport, and amid chaotic scenes the convoy was immobilised. In a moment caught for posterity by the cameras, Hill jumped out of the team bus and started walking down the street below the hotel bellowing at the media vehicles to get out of the way. Eventually the convoy got going, and for the next 25 minutes a motley assortment of cars and buses careered its way through the traffic jams, narrowly avoiding several high-speed crashes along the way. The Socceroos made it to the ground for their date with destiny, but without a lot of time to spare.

Finally, on a crisp winter afternoon before 127 998 men and two women (Hill's girlfriend and an intrepid Australian backpacker), it was time for the talking to stop. Action was to speak a lot louder than words. Iran, who had established a new world record with a 17–0 win over the Maldives in an early qualifier, would fight for their World Cup future against the team in green and gold, the home team spurred on by an atmosphere that was both intimidating and exhilarating—the crowd later described by Venables as the most vocal he had ever experienced. (And this from a man who had spent a season on the bench at Barcelona's famous Nou Camp.) In the context of Australia's chequered World Cup history, this was as big as it could get.

The possibilities loomed even larger for the Socceroos after a superbly crafted goal converted by Kewell just 20 minutes into the match. A hesitant, nervous Iranian defence was sliced apart when a Horvat free kick was chested down by Viduka and his lay off dropped the ball into the path of the Socceroos' youngest player. On his World Cup debut, Kewell made a difficult chance look simple. The crowd fell silent. Kewell sprinted to the corner flag with his arms outstretched, and was jumped upon by Slater. For the Socceroos it was the perfect start.

Gradually, almost imperceptibly, Iran clawed their way back into the contest.

The Australian flanks, particularly the left side, began to be exposed by the speed and touch of players such as Mahdavikia, Azizi, Mansourian and Saadavi. By the 30-minute mark, the pendulum had swung towards the home side. A goal from Azizi just before the break, after Bosnich had produced a string of excellent saves, was just reward. The crowd went berserk. The noise level went up another decibel. As the Socceroos gratefully retreated to the sanctuary of their dressing-room at the interval, they knew their character was about to be examined. In detail.

But they survived—somehow. The rutted pitch caused Australian hearts to flutter every time the ball came into the penalty area, but the defence held firm, and when they were beaten Bosnich came to the rescue. It was a matter of hanging on. And they did. The Italian referee, much to Venables' relief, barely added a minute of extra time. At the whistle, the players embraced. It had ended 1–1. A draw, and a precious away goal. And this in the most testing environment imaginable. In 90 pulsating minutes, the team had grown-up. The World Cup, after 23 years of frustration, was just one step away. 'This will make us feel good about the second game,' said Venables. 'I've got to be happy with that.' As the team winged its way over the Persian Gulf later that night, the players couldn't help but feel optimistic about the future. The hardest part was over. The job had been done. Now their fate was in their own hands.

The nation, certainly, felt the same way. By the time the squad touched down at Melbourne's Tullamarine Airport 36 hours later, the Socceroos were headline news. Front and back pages, prime time bulletins, hourly radio updates. It was unprecedented. The country was awash with soccermania. A nation that has always loved a winner embraced the Socceroos. And none more than Kewell, the baby-faced assassin who was fast developing into a world-class talent. Other players who had spent their entire careers in the shadows leapt into the limelight. Managers, agents, publicists descended. Ghosted columns appeared. Almost overnight, soccer had pierced the sporting consciousness. Tickets sales, already strong, gathered momentum. There was talk of a sell-out at the 98 000-capacity Melbourne Cricket Ground. There was talk of millions of dollars flooding into the coffers in sponsorships, television rights and kit deals. This was the moment when the sport would finally wake from its slumber. Twenty-nine November 1997 would be remembered as the day Australian soccer came of age. Everyone seemed certain of it. Iran, of course, had other ideas.

Venables did his best to keep the lid on the euphoria. Media access, restricted as it had been overseas, was even more tightly controlled in Melbourne. And whenever

THE BIG ONE

he got the opportunity to say it, the coach reminded the nation that the job was only half-done. With Lazaridis regarded as a certainty to return to the side, and with the MCG pitch an infinite improvement on Tehran, there was every reason to believe the Socceroos would improve on their subdued showing away from home. When Okon returned the following day from a flying visit to Sydney to announce his specialist had given him the all-clear, all the key indicators were pointing in the right direction: to France.

To keep the players' minds on the job, Venables elected to train behind closed doors in the 48 hours before the match. Iran, by sharp contrast, made their sessions open to all and sundry. Coach Valdier Vierra, so approachable and quotable in Tehran, continued to look remarkably relaxed as he approached the biggest game of his journeyman career. As he alighted the team bus on a blistering 40-degree evening at Knights Park in North Sunshine, Vierra obligingly dealt with every request for an interview and photo as his players changed in the dressing-room. Even after the training session started, the coach strolled the touchline, cigarette in hand, chatting to journalists and supporters. Hundreds of Iranian fans cheered every touch by the players, but particularly Bagheri. The presence of the team's most influential player visibly lifted morale. He had arrived separately after a taxing 40-hour journey from Germany, where he was playing his club football, and was introduced to Vierra for the first time just three days before the match. Bagheri's absence over the previous three weeks through suspension had coincided with Vierra's elevation to the coaching position. But although he had never seen him play, Vierra had no hesitation in naming Bagheri in his side. 'Seventy million people tell me I must pick him, so who am I to say no?' he joked.

The ready smile on Vierra's face reflected the mood in the Iranian camp: quiet confidence, belief in their own ability, and contentment that all the pressure was on their opponents. Away from home, and at the end of a punishing campaign that had stretched for five months and involved weeks of travel, Iran accepted they were underdogs, particularly after being held by the Socceroos in Tehran. Clearly, it was a status they were happy to accept. It was a status Australia had, historically, regarded as their own.

But the Socceroos were underdogs no more. The hype, the media frenzy, heightened expectations. And with it came the ticket sales. By the morning of the match, a sell-out was all but guaranteed. Nobody had ever dreamed a soccer match would be able to fill the cavernous MCG. It would almost double the previous highest attendance record, set over 30 years earlier when New South Wales played

Everton at the Sydney Cricket Ground. It was destined, in every sense, to be a night to remember. The burning question was, for whom?

The fans came by the trainload, the planeload, the carload, the busload. A charter flight of Iranians from the United States arrived the day before the game. The 631st and final qualifier for France 98 had captured worldwide attention. There would be live television coverage in 90 countries, a further 58 nations taking delayed coverage. Melbourne, the capital of the world as far as Australian football and cricket is concerned, had opened its arms to the round-ball game. And soccer relished it in return. Shopfronts in trendy Chapel Street were decorated with posters. Pubs around South Yarra, Carlton, Richmond and St Kilda were full by lunchtime on the day of the game. There was a sense of purpose, and history, in the air. The previous night, the 1974 Socceroos had been brought together for the first time by Soccer Australia. A few hours before the game, they were joined by a host of other former internationals at the Bluestone Cafe on St Kilda Road. For the first time, there was a feeling of pride, of belonging, of unity. A multitude of generations—Hammy McMeecham, Dennis Yaager, Roy Blitz, Ted Smith, Bill Rice, Yakka Banovic, Tony Henderson, Theo Selemides, Ken Murphy, Gary Cole, John Kosmina, Eddie Krncevic, Steve O'Connor, Garry McDowall, Robbie Dunn—all shared experiences over a beer or two. All agreed on one thing: the worth of a green and gold shirt. And all hoping that this time it would work out all right.

It should have. But it didn't. Tragically so. Unbelievably so. Unfairly so. Few people are yet able to comprehend just what occurred at the MCG on that late spring evening. What the 85 000 crowd saw, and what a record domestic television audience saw, was one team totally dominate another. Wave after wave of a green and gold tide lapped the Iranian goal guarded by Abedzadeh. Aurelio Vidmar could have had a hat-trick inside 12 minutes. A shot from Kewell was rocketing towards the target until it was deflected off the head an Iranian defender who knew nothing about it. Finally, Kewell scored, and justice seemed certain to prevail. There was only one team in it. Rarely had an Australian team been so totally in control. Rarely had the Socceroos played with such verve and imagination. But instead of being four goals up at half-time, they were only one. And that left a glimmer of hope for their outclassed opponents.

That glimmer seemed to disappear when Vidmar, finally and deservedly, grabbed Australia's second goal early in the second half. The boisterous, chanting, screaming gallery—surely the best atmosphere ever generated by an Australian crowd of any sporting persuasion—were preparing to celebrate a momentous occasion. But then

THE BIIG OINE

the momentum was lost when a spectator ran from behind the Iranian goal and jumped on the net, causing it to break free from the crossbar. The man, who only a few weeks earlier had run onto the finishing straight during the running of the Melbourne Cup, was led away by security staff, pelted with beer and fruit as he went. Play was held up for nine minutes while staff refastened the net. Perhaps it was then that the players began to picture France in their mind's eye. Whatever the case, they lost concentration. Fatally so. A warning shot was fired across the bows when Azizi forced Bosnich into a smart save. But the warning was not heeded. Azizi chased another through ball down the right; the Socceroos made a mess of the clearance. Craig Moore didn't kick it away, it rebounded to Azizi, and his cutback found the unmarked Bagheri, who slotted it into an empty net. Television replays later confirmed that Azizi was in an offside position when he crossed to Bagheri, but none of the players, coaching staff, media or spectators saw it that way at the time. Things were starting to get nerve-racking. Surely the Socceroos couldn't blow it from here?

Just a few minutes later, Tobin and Horvat attempted to play the offside trap, and it was sprung. Azizi held his nerve and guided his shot past Bosnich. The score was 2–2, Iran in the box seat on the away goals rule. Two goals inside four minutes, both the products of woeful Australian defending. Nobody, but nobody, could believe what they had just seen. Iran could scarcely believe their luck. Venables finally moved his substitutes off the bench, but the horse had bolted. Over the frantic final minutes, Arnold twice went close to putting the Socceroos through. But it was never destined to be. The whistle came from Hungarian referee Sandor Puhl, and it was over. Aggregate scores 3–3, but Iran through to France 98 for scoring twice away from home. Back in Tehran, millions of people poured into the streets. A national holiday was declared. It was the country's biggest celebration since the end of the war with Iraq. Inside the MCG, 5000 Iranian fans embraced their players. Vierra was chaired off the field on the shoulders on his team. Mayhem.

It was cruel. A team that had lost three games during the qualifying stages would be going to the World Cup at the expense of a team that had not lost a game. Four minutes aside, the Socceroos had comprehensively outplayed their opponents. But those four minutes were the ones that mattered. Four years went down the drain.

Questions, not surprisingly, were asked. Why hadn't Venables made the substitutions earlier, when the team was still leading 2–0 and some players were tiring, visibly? Why had the defence suddenly, inexplicably, decided to play the offside trap? Why had Milan Ivanovic, the lynchpin of the Australia defence for eight years, been left on the sidelines when his influence was so obviously needed? Why had the team had such limited preparation in the two months leading up to the games? Why? Why? Why?

These were all legitimate queries, and Venables would ultimately accept that mistakes had been made. But the truth was, Australia should have won the game by a cricket score. The truth was the Socceroos fell on their own sword. It was the unkindest cut of all.

CHAPTER 12

TEARS FOR FEARS

IT WAS A COUPLE OF HOURS INTO THE LAST DAY of spring, 1997. But if there was love in the air, it was lost on Robbie Slater. Around him, hundreds of late-night revellers hawked themselves and their intentions around the 'Heat' nightclub, part of Melbourne's massive new casino complex. But Slater was oblivious to the commotion. Slumped in his seat, he stared intermittently at the glass he cradled in his right hand. When he wasn't trying to discover the meaning of life in the bottom of his appropriately named Victoria Bitter, he was staring, blankly, straight ahead. The truth was, the meaning of life—at that precise moment in his 33-year-old life—was nowhere to be found. His wife, Nathalie, and his children, Victoria and Tom, were on the other side of the world, in the south of England. Amid the heaving, sweating, swaying mass of humanity which surrounded him, he had never felt so lonely, so depressed. He wanted his family, he wanted to hold them tight, and he wanted to cry—to sob, uncontrollably. He wanted to seek refuge, to seek comfort, in their arms; to seek answers, perhaps.

But the answers were as elusive as the dream. Why? Why? Why? The thought kept bouncing around his head. And the only answer that kept coming back was that there was no answer; there was only the harsh, unforgiving reality. But Slater did not want to digest the twisted knot of frustration that lay deep within his stomach. Not just yet. He took another sip. And he stared ahead.

Graham Arnold was standing directly in his line of vision. He had never had a better mate in his life. They had shared so much in the decade or so since they'd first met as teammates at Sydney United. Their careers had taken them to disparate parts of the world, but never more than a few weeks had passed between phone calls. They had had arguments, sure. They sometimes complained about each other to others. But it was never serious. Their relationship, their friendship, remained as strong as it had ever been. Slater knew that perhaps the only person in the world who truly, genuinely, knew what he was going through right now was a few metres away. He got to his feet. He put his arm around his mate. There were no tears, although both men were crying inside. There were not even words. Nothing had to be said. And then 'Arnie' and 'Bulldog', the great inseparables, looked at each other—looked back in time and saw years of shared experiences pass before their eyes—and shouted the immortal words as loud as they could. In unison and, this time, with conviction. 'The end of an era!'. And it was.

Retirement is a prospect that all sportsmen must face eventually. But this didn't alter the pain and anguish that Slater and Arnold were suffering. For Arnold, four World Cup campaigns and twelve years with the national team had yielded no reward. For Slater, it was three campaigns and a decade in the green and gold. As the darkness outside retreated before the first shafts of daylight, reality dawned with it. It was the first day of the rest of their lives. Things would never, could never, be the same again. It was over.

Yet if it was an intensely personal grief for the two old warhorses of the Socceroo team, it was a grief shared to varying degrees by many others and by a nation. Only a matter of hours before, 80 000 parochial fans had sat in stony, disbelieving silence as the shrill whistle of Hungarian referee Sandor Puhl had signalled the end of another of Australia's increasingly frustrating quests to qualify for the World Cup. Tears were shed by many in the huge, circular bowl that is the Melbourne Cricket Ground. Many were first-timers attracted by the massive hype and publicity which had preceded the deciding match against Iran. But there were plenty of others, too, who had been involved in the game, who believed in the game, who loved the game. There were former Socceroos from as far back as the 1950s. There were former coaches, officials and referees. There were people who had never risen to greater heights than the local suburban park and the local suburban team. There were people who had risen way beyond that, people who had emigrated from distant nations where soccer is the elixir of the masses, but who had grown to love this country as their own. Greeks, Croats, Italians, Serbs, Poles, Scots, Turks, Czechs, Vietnamese—the melting pot that is multicultural Australia had come to support the green and gold cause. And who knows how many tears were shed in living

Previous page: Australia's Ernie Tapai competes for the ball in the World Cup qualifying match against Iran at the Melbourne Cricket Ground. SEAN GARNSWORTHY/SPORTING PIX
Above: The fans cheer as Australia scores a second goal against Iran. CLAYTON/THE SYDNEY MORNING HERALD

Previous page: Australian socceroo Robbie Slater. TONY FEDER/SPORTING PIX
Above: A disappointed Steve Horvat leaves the ground after losing to Iran in the World Cup qualifying match held in Melbourne. SEAN GARNSWORTHY/SPORTING PIX

T/E/A/R/S F/O/R F/E/A/R/S

rooms around the country, or by expatriates in any of the 90 countries throughout the world that took live pictures of the match beamed via satellite from a van parked on a grass verge outside the northern end of the ground. They may even have been crying inside the van, for all we know. Harry Michaels, the director, has been known to live his soccer as passionately as anyone else. For soccer is a passion first and a sport second. And no matter who you were or where you were, the sense of belonging was pervasive. The national team had never been owned by any individual, it had only ever been owned by everyone. Which gave everyone the right to share in the experience. And for most, it was an experience impossible to forget.

Ten-twelve p.m., 29 November 1997. The giant scoreboard at the MCG remains illuminated with the fateful missive Australia 2, Iran 2. The Socceroos are out of the World Cup. Again. The real scoreboard makes even more sobering reading—nine World Cup campaigns, only one success. It was the sixth failed attempt in a row, and unquestionably the most disheartening. Twenty minutes earlier, the scoreline had been full of exciting promise: Australia 2, Iran 0. The 85 000 strong crowd—the biggest ever to watch a soccer match in this country—had been chanting, singing, screaming, laughing. Raw, unashamed patriotism hung in the still night air. And it was shared, too, by the 5000 Iranian fans in the ground, split into two main groups behind either goal. But this was to be Australia's night, or so everyone thought. For the Socceroos, France 98 beckoned invitingly over the horizon. Surely, finally, this was it. But it wasn't, of course. Two goals inside four minutes and the dream evaporated as quickly as it took for Khodadad Azizi to beat the offside trap, scythe into the open space, and score.

It was not that the Socceroos had lost, because they hadn't. It was not that the team had not played well, because it had. It was not that Iranians were the better team; they weren't. Rather, it was the surprise, the sheer speed, of the demise which cut so deep. It was because the dream had been snatched away with the stealth of a burglar in the dead of night. It just seemed so... well... unfair. That is why the experience was so debilitating. So devastating. So disheartening. That is why the sense of loss was overwhelming, overpowering. Australia could have, should have, been going to the World Cup. But Iran—a clever team representing a proud nation—would be going instead.

Nobody could quite believe what had happened. Hours later, as the drinks gradually dulled the pain, the players were no closer to grasping just what had occurred. Yes, there had been an awful defensive mix-up which allowed Iran to score their first goal. No, Steve Horvat and Alex Tobin should never have pushed up in a forlorn attempt to play an offside trap which had never been an integral part of the tactical plan. Yes, Aurelio Vidmar should have put away more of the chances that fell his way in Australia's withering opening burst. This was the stark evidence which would be replayed over and over again in the minds of the players, and before a worldwide audience on television. These were, indeed, the defining moments when the best-laid plans went horribly wrong. But they were not the only explanation. The real question remains unanswered, as it will in the days and years to come. Why?

Stan Lazaridis, who remained prostrate on the MCG turf for 20 minutes after the final whistle, could scarcely comprehend the enormity of what had occurred. Robbie Hooker, not even named as a substitute, was simply inconsolable. Everything he had ever aspired to from his days as a junior on Sydney's North Shore 20 years before had evaporated in a flash. Never had the future looked so bleak. 'It's all right for you blokes,' he told the overseas-based players. 'I'm stuck here [playing for Sydney United]. This was my last chance.' Yet despite the general despair, the words of mid-fielder Craig Foster—uttered to an interviewer seconds after the end of the game—hinted that life must, and would, go on. 'We win as a team, and we lose as a team,' he had said. And on this night the team was trying its hardest to bond in defeat.

Back at the hotel, just across the road from the now-darkened silhouette of the MCG, the other half of the equation, the coaching staff, were pondering the same question—Why?—and having the same trouble finding an answer. And there was one man who was troubled more than most.

Terry Venables. El Tel. Or Oz Tel as he had been coined by the Australian press. One of the biggest names in world football. Accustomed to the biggest stages, and the biggest players. But, as he approached the peak of his coaching career, his biggest ambition—the World Cup—was still unfulfilled. As a player, Venables had been a couple of years too young when England won the Jules Rimet trophy in 1966. Although capped at every level by his country, he was destined not to make it to the only tournament that truly matters. For awhile it seemed he might get there as England coach. Handed the post after Graham Taylor had failed so spectacularly to get the team to the 1994 tournament in the United States, much had been expected of Venables. He had long been regarded as one of England's most astute man-managers and tacticians—his education rounded off by his successful experience in Spain with FC Barcelona. There was almost universal

TEARS FOR FEARS

acclaim when he took charge of England's moribund national team. And in many ways, he did not disappoint. Venables guided England to the semi-finals of the 1996 European Championships, taking players like Paul Ince, Alan Shearer and Teddy Sheringham to new levels in the process. But by the time England were bundled out of the tournament by their arch rivals Germany at Wembley, Venables was already on his way. He had resigned six months earlier on a matter of principle—annoyed that his bosses at the Football Association lacked the faith to extend his contract past Euro 96 until after the tournament was over.

It was a supreme irony, therefore, that his successor, Glenn Hoddle, would prosper from his legacy. A month before the Socceroos faced their final hurdle against Iran, England qualified for the World Cup. Venables would only say he was proud to have played a hand. But that was when his new team, Australia, had every reason to believe it would be joining England in France. Much was made of the possibility that Venables might even coach the Socceroos against his old team. But, of course, fate played another cruel hand. A man who had so often gambled on the big decisions in his life was to lose out, again. It was a thought which must have occupied his mind in the hours after Australia's incredible implosion at the MCG.

Venables was supposed to have been the insurance. He was supposed to have guaranteed that after so many glorious failures, so many near-misses, this time the Socceroos would get over the line. Nothing had been spared to make it so. Venables was to be handsomely rewarded for his part-time role. He was to be given everything he wanted, whenever he wanted it. Distractions which usually go with the territory—sponsors, media, other coaches—were kept to the barest minimum. Nothing was to compromise his mission. First-class travel, seven-star hotels, any number of back-up staff. No matter that the game could not, in truth, afford it. When you want the best, you have to pay for it. That had been the rationale of Soccer Australia chairman David Hill when he had convinced Venables to put pen to paper twelve months earlier. But the beauty of football is that money doesn't win games or put the ball into the back of the net. There may have been three million good reasons, each of them a dollar, as to why Australia should have made it to the World Cup. But, ultimately, none of them counted.

'I don't think I've ever played in such a cruel game,' Venables told the after-match press conference. 'We had looked as good a side as any you will see in the finals.' But, of course, no-one will ever know.

It was never supposed to have ended like this. For months the momentum had been building towards the right conclusion. As the Socceroos swept through a series of friendlies in the early part of the year, humbled their opponents in the Oceania section of the World Cup campaign, and then warmed-up for the play-offs with an emphatic victory in another friendly international in Tunisia, it seemed nothing could stand in their way. Australia's demise was something Venables, as much as anyone else, had least expected. For Slater it was particularly painful. Although raised in the western suburbs of Sydney, he had married a French woman and had spent the best years of his career playing in the city of Lens, close to the Belgian border. Lens had been selected as one of the host cities for France 98. Slater was desperate to return to his adopted home, in triumph, with the Socceroos. He was hugely popular in Lens, where he still retained a fan club. One of his green and gold shirts hung on the wall of the football museum at the Stade Felix Bolleart. But that was as close as Australia would get to a presence in the World Cup of 1998. Iran had seen to that. True enough, the Socceroos made Iran look, for large parts of the game, second-rate. True enough, they established some kind of record in failing to qualify without losing a game. But this was scant consolation.

It was not only the players who suffered in the aftermath. The image of a glassy-eyed John Warren, the former Socceroo captain, unable to utter more than a few token words in his role as television expert was especially poignant. Warren was not alone in his desolation. Letters poured into newspapers and magazines from fans stunned to the core by what had happened. One such came from a Sydney resident, David Payne, in a fax sent to the *Sydney Morning Herald*.

> 'Before I left the MCG I went to where the Iranian fans were celebrating down by the pitch. I thought that being around happy people would help. The people I spoke to were lovely about their unexpected good fortune. My brother said at the time that I was going through denial. I cannot remember all the stages in the grieving process, but I think I eventually skipped anger and went on to acceptance. Why did it feel so much like bereavement?'

The result was unexpected, too, for the coach of the victorious team. Valdier Vierra, a Brazilian, had only been in charge of Iran for the three weeks leading up to the game. He had started the year believing he would be going to the World Cup finals with Costa Rica. But such are the vagaries of football. He ended the year having fulfilled his ambition, but with a team from another hemisphere, another culture, another heritage. Vierra, who has spent his life in pursuit of football's most elusive dream, was magnanimous enough, generous enough, to put his crowning achievement into an honest perspective.

'I'm happy on one hand, but on the other I'm also sad because Australian soccer loses a lot. There are millions of kids here who want to play, and for Australia to go to the finals would have given the game here a great push. If somebody had to win this game, it wasn't me. Before I'm a coach I'm a football lover, and football is what Australia played today. They didn't let us see anything of the ball in the first half. It was like coming to Melbourne in the summer and not seeing the sun. But God has helped us, that's for sure.'

Certainly there had been no divine intervention on the Socceroo's behalf. The luck that so often decides winners from losers deserted Australia in its hour of need. Yet if the line between success and failure was, ultimately, as fine as a gossamer thread, the cumulative effect of another failed World Cup campaign created almost as much anger as sympathy. Much of it had to do with the autocratic leadership style of Hill. He was the one who had gone out and recruited Venables at a time when many felt the cause would have been better served by a local coach taking charge. He was the one who sanctioned the outlay of millions of dollars to finance a campaign which spared no expense. Venables and his players were treated in the manner of first world teams such as Brazil, Germany, England and Argentina. The difference was that these teams had earned the right to be feted. They had won World Cups and were regular visitors to finals. So when the Socceroos fell out of the frame, a backlash was inevitable. In the minds of those disenchanted souls who felt they had been marginalised in the decision-making process, Hill deserved to be held personally accountable for the failure. Within hours there were rumblings about a vote of no confidence. There was talk of a clean sweep of the board. Hill had gambled on the Venables appointment and had lost. He had to go.

If the reaction was short-sighted, it was perhaps understandable. So much hope and emotion had been invested. Many of the traditional stakeholders felt an immense sense of loss that a so-called interloper, Hill, had taken control of their game, and had handed over control of its most precious asset, the national team, to another interloper, Venables. For heaven's sake, he was even allowed to continue living in London while coaching the Socceroos. So when it all came crashing down, there were bound to be recriminations. But Hill was tough enough, and strong enough, to ride out the storm. Only once did his facade of composure crack, when he launched a scathing attack on Club Marconi's president, Tony Labbozzetta, a prominent member of the old guard. Labbozzetta and Hill were the bitterest of enemies long before Venables came onto the scene. Their public slanging match in the days that followed the World Cup disaster was viewed as merely the latest instalment of a long-running personal feud. Those within the game knew the score.

The Socceroos, had been denied a place in the main event. For many, there would never be the opportunity to make amends. For Venables, however, there would be other opportunities, with other teams, in other countries. He had come, he had seen, but he had not conquered. The script written by Hill, with Venables in centre stage, was to sign off without the happy ending. It had all been so different at the start.

CHAPTER 3

DESERT STORM

IN THE HOLLOW, DESOLATE MINUTES THAT FOLLOWED the World Cup failure, a host of Socceroos contemplated retirement, including some of the younger members of the squad. The thought of kicking another ball, any ball, seemed immensely unappealing. It felt as though the world had come crashing down, so bitter was the pill to swallow. But life would go on, of course, and careers would be put back on track. Within 48 hours of the final whistle at the MCG, all but veteran Graham Arnold had recanted their private declarations of retirement. In other circumstances, perhaps, a few more players might have made good the threat. But the truth was there was no time for genuine reflection. Reasoned, researched decisions would have to wait. Goodbye World Cup, hello Confederations Cup. Within seven days of the cataclysm in Melbourne, the Socceroos were required to report for duty back in the Middle East. Not Tehran or Dubai this time, but Riyadh, the capital of Saudi Arabia and venue for the third edition of what had developed into a mini-World Cup.

Mentally, it was a huge ask. The hangover from the World Cup lingered on. Players retreated to their clubs to lick their wounds, but some couldn't sleep. Robbie Slater rang a friend in Australia in the middle of the night to unburden his tortured soul. Aurelio Vidmar went home to Adelaide to seek comfort with family and friends. Why? Why? Why? Five days after the match, the World Cup draw was held at the Stade Velodrome in Marseilles. Iran were grouped with Yugoslavia, the US and Germany. The players couldn't help but assess the opposition, work out the permutations, and wonder why it couldn't have been them. Perhaps the best therapy was at hand. Perhaps playing in the Confederations Cup was the perfect release after all. A squad of 21 was named, and all of them turned up. Lazaridis, who had flown straight from Melbourne to London to play a midweek game against Crystal Palace, even went head-to-head with his manager at West Ham, Harry Redknapp. The manager insisted Lazaridis was too tired to go to Saudi Arabia. Venables was quickly on the phone to suggest to Redknapp—an old mate— otherwise. And Lazaridis staunchly defied his manager and demanded he go. He went, and there was nothing West Ham could do to stop him.

This was the first 'official' Confederations Cup, and FIFA had the power to spring the players from their clubs. It was not something that was widely appreciated in Europe, where FIFA officials were required to mediate with several Italian clubs who had wanted to keep hold of their stable of Brazilian stars. Ultimately FIFA was to prevail, and Brazil ended up sending its top team to the Middle East. But the future of the Confederations Cup—particularly its timing—remains the subject of heated debate.

Heated it was, too, in Riyadh where eight teams—the champions of the six confederations plus the World Cup winners (Brazil) and the hosts (Saudi Arabia)— gathered for what amounted to a pre-World Cup. Four of the competing teams— Brazil, Saudi, Mexico and South Africa—had qualified for France 98 and viewed the tournament as invaluable preparation. The Socceroos, by contrast, had to share the dubious distinction of being cast among the World Cup also-rans with Uruguay, Czech Republic and the United Arab Emirates. But at least that meant they had something to prove.

The King Fahd Stadium is a spectacular edifice to the unimaginable wealth of the Saudi royal family. Nicknamed 'The Marble of the Desert', it cost $900 million to build. Its eye-catching design includes grandstands encircled by a giant tented structure, while underneath the pitch a reservoir of 8000 cubic metres of water has been filled to ensure the playing surface remains lush all-year round. It was the perfect venue for a competition of such stature. The Socceroos may have arrived as rank outsiders, but ultimately they would do justice to their opulent surroundings, more so given the overwhelming sense of uncertainty that surrounded the squad. Nobody knew whether Venables would be staying on. Nobody knew how quickly the Socceroos would be able to recover from their World Cup trauma in a daunting group which contained Brazil, Mexico and Saudi Arabia—all at full strength.

The players wondered about their own futures, too. Eventually—midway

D/E/S/E/R/T S/T/O/R/M

through the tournament—Slater would join his best friend Arnold in announcing his retirement. 'I thought about quitting after the MCG game, but when you're full of emotion it is a dangerous time to make a decision,' he said. 'After we were eliminated, I was gutted. It was the worst feeling I've had in my life. But now I feel right about it [retirement]. I've achieved all of my goals, apart from one. I've always said everyone lives in their own era, and unfortunately mine didn't involve going to the World Cup.' And so it was, at the end of a decorated international career which included three World Cup campaigns and the indelible memory of being embraced and admired by Diego Maradona, 'the bulldog' had decided to call it quits. The dressing-room, certainly, would never be the same again.

Yet if the Confederations Cup was to mark the beginning of a period of transition for the national team, one constant remained intact. Ever since 1967, when the Socceroos had travelled to Vietnam, major tournaments involving Australia had been regularly interrupted by pay disputes. This was to be no exception.

A year earlier, when the Socceroos had qualified for the Confederations Cup by winning the Oceania Nations Cup final against Tahiti, the players' union believed it had reached agreement with the national body. A profit-sharing deal to cover both the World Cup campaign and Confederations Cup in Riyadh had been accepted in principle by Soccer Australia's chief executive, David Woolley. But his chairman, David Hill, simply refused to sanction it. When the home-based Socceroos gathered under Venables for the first time two months later, they discovered they had been duped. Angered by the slight, they voted 21–1 in favour of a strike during the four nations tournament, but eventually backed down from the threat when Hill pledged further, serious, negotiation. Those talks never materialised, and instead Hill presented the Socceroos—this time only the overseas-based players—with a schedule of payments a few hours after the friendly in Budapest three months later. The squad was informed the offer was non-negotiable. Unwisely, the players neglected to call in their union. Eight months later, with the World Cup campaign in tatters and their own payments seriously eroded as a result, the players decided they would not be undersold. With Hill proudly claiming Soccer Australia had made a $2 million profit on the World Cup decider in Melbourne, and with FIFA suddenly announcing that prizemoney in Saudi Arabia would be significantly increased, the players made their stand.

When the squad arrived in Riyadh, the players were quick to meet with Hill to ask that the deal be re-negotiated. They had missed out on bonuses totalling $30 000 after failing to qualify for the World Cup, and many of the squad members were looking at making only $14 500 (before tax) out of the year. For some, this was barely a week's wages at club level. If not for the unexpected upswing in Soccer Australia's fortunes, the players might have been content. But when it became abundantly clear that the federation was about to benefit from a multimillion dollar windfall, the players felt they deserved better compensation. This was the point put to Hill at the Mariott Hotel in Riyadh, but it was a point the chairman refused to accept. The meeting only served to pour fuel on the fire. In typically aggressive style, Hill let it be known that there would be no renegotiation.

The players would not be cowed. They responded by voting 18–3 to boycott training for the two days leading up to the opening match of the tournament, against Mexico. Some had considered not playing at all, but with the tournament sanctioned as a FIFA event the players appreciated that a strike would rebound disastrously on the nation. Australia might even be banned from international competition, as it had been in the early 1960s. Nonetheless, the mood remained steadfastly determined. Having backed down early in the year, the players were resolved not to buckle again. They were virtually united against Hill.

> 'It's been non-negotiable from day one,' a senior player later told AAP. 'We've been treated like animals. It's been crap, unprofessional garbage. There has never even been a willingness to listen. David Hill told us: "If you don't like it, strike. I dare you." Now the players are getting as militant as he is. It's blown up in his face because he has refused all along to deal with it. Even now he's avoiding players, saying he's offended and upset and won't speak to us. He runs away when he sees you.'

Venables, for his part, sympathised with the players, but, as had been the case during the four nations tournament at the start of the year, he declined to become involved. And Hill was glad of that, for the chairman had other pertinent matters to discuss with his coach—namely whether he would agree to stay on. Just minutes after the World Cup demise in Melbourne, Hill had told Venables, and then the world, that he would be offering the coach a new contract. And his prime purpose for being in Riyadh was to try to bed it down. Indeed, two days after the tournament got underway Hill announced that Venables had agreed in principle to remain with the Socceroos until the next World Cup campaign in 2001. But the statement was short of detail and, significantly, it contained no quotes from Venables. The reality was that the announcement was vastly premature. Venables had so many other offers on his plate that he was not ready to commit himself to anything yet.

D/E/S/E/R/T S/T/O/R/M

In the midst of such an uncertain environment, the results the Socceroos went on to attain at the Confederations Cup were a remarkable achievement. It was also a painful reminder that but for the catastrophic four minutes at the MCG, the Socceroos would have deservedly qualified for the World Cup, and would have performed with distinction once they got there. The gap between Australia and the top echelon of football nations had narrowed to such an extent, and while nothing could compensate for the World Cup failure, the players in Riyadh felt strongly they had something to prove; not just to the rest of the football world, either. In the context of their industrial dispute, they wanted to prove to their own paymasters that they were worthy of more respect. That they succeeded in their mission remains an enduring testament not only to their ability, but to their character. This was not a team that was prepared to be taken for granted.

For the opening match against Mexico, Venables was forced to make three changes to the side which had played Iran less than two weeks earlier. Bosnich had arrived late in Saudi Arabia after helping his club team, Aston Villa, into the quarterfinals of the UEFA Cup. He was rested in preference to his long-time understudy, Kalac. Up front, Kewell was nursing a nagging knee injury and the opportunity was handed to John Aloisi, who had been in good scoring form for Portsmouth in the English first division. And stopper Craig Moore had damaged his ankle in the dying minutes of the World Cup qualifier in Melbourne, and had been left out of the squad altogether because of the injury. Moore's Glasgow Rangers teammate Tony Vidmar manned the centre of defence in his place.

Despite the changes, despite the psychological scars they carried into the tournament, the Socceroos barely skipped a beat. Mexico, ranked 11th in the world, had sacked coach Bora Milutinovic, even though he had guided them into the World Cup, and were playing under a new coach, Manuel Lapuente, for the first time. They were formidable opponents, nonetheless, and were widely expected to account for the Socceroos.

The Australians had other ideas. After a solid beginning, the Socceroos took the lead with a typically penetrating burst by Viduka, who finished bravely in front of the goalkeeper to score only his second goal for the national team. Just after the break the underdogs extended their lead, this time Aloisi finishing a sweeping move in spectacular, muscular fashion. The Mexicans equalised from the penalty spot after Kalac brought down substitute Luis Hernandez, and—momentarily—the images of squandering a two-goal lead against Iran resurfaced. But the Socceroos held their nerve and regrouped. Right at the death, substitute Damien Mori added a third to secure a richly deserved victory. It was the first time Australia had beaten Mexico in four outings, and it opened up the group. It also helped to exorcise a few demons, as Venables was quick to emphasise.

'The Iran game was a freak point. I've never seen anything like it,' he remarked. 'We did everything right in both matches until we suffered that cruel fate. It was just a wicked blow. But the main thing is we've gotten over it. We dug in harder [against Mexico] and turned it around. We haven't had much time to get over that horrendous blow in Melbourne, so in the circumstances I thought the boys did exceptionally well.' In coach-speak, that meant Venables was enormously impressed with the character of his team. What he also knew, and the rest of the world did not, was the backdrop of ill-feeling over the pay issue. The news would not break for another few days. In the meantime, the Socceroos had to contend with the daunting prospect of playing Brazil.

Ronaldo, Romario, Bebeto, Denilson, Juninho, Leonardo, Roberto Carlos. All destined to star in France 98. All contenders for any World XI. The $200 million team. The best in the world. And, like the Socceroos, enjoying a record-breaking run. Australia's achievement of 14 consecutive wins, which had ended with the draw in Tehran, had just been matched by Brazil with a 3–0 win over Saudi Arabia in their opening match of the Confederations Cup. A win over the Socceroos would establish a new mark, although it was not widely known at the time.

In the only previous meetings between the two nations, all played in 1988, Brazil had won 1–0, 2–0 and 3–0. Romario had scored in each game, including a hat-trick in the last encounter at the Seoul Olympics. And he was here again in Riyadh, rejuvenated after a typically turbulent few years at club level, and waiting to pounce. The 'little bastard', as former national coach Frank Arok had admiringly labelled him, was back to haunt the Socceroos. Or was he? When the two teams were led onto the pitch before an audience of just over 10 000 fans, Romario was listed among the substitutes. And there, on the bench, he was destined to stay.

Coach Mario Zagallo would come to rue the decision, for a striking partnership which boasted the diverse talents of Ronaldo and Bebeto was to draw a blank. Pummelled for most of the game, with Bosnich forced into a succession of saves, the Socceroos hung on grimly. The ageless Milan Ivanovic, restored to the defence after his controversial omission against Iran, was imperious. And Viduka even had the audacity to spurn a gilt-edged chance. Two weeks after being eliminated from the World Cup, Australia, ranked 32nd in the world, had held no. 1 ranked Brazil to a 0–0 draw. Unbelievable.

D/E/S/E/R/T S/T/O/R/M

It was the first time in 28 matches, played over two years, that the World Cup holders had been kept scoreless. It was a truly magnificent result—the best ever achieved by the Socceroos. Only a 4–1 win over Argentina (in 1988) and a 1–0 win over Yugoslavia (also in 1988) compared. The national team was back on the front pages, this time for the right reasons. The Socceroos had again demonstrated that the Iran result had been an awful aberration. For the fifth time in a year the Socceroos had played a team that had qualified for the World Cup, and they had yet to lose a match. 'The longer it went on, the less we looked like losing,' said Venables. 'We have a lot of respect for Brazil, but you've got to be careful that respect doesn't go over the top into fear.'

Bosnich, who threw himself all over his penalty area, was certainly fearless. He was also philosophical. Echoing the mood of the dressing-room, he said, 'It was one of our best performances, but we would gladly trade it for a place in the World Cup.'

But they would have to make do with a place in the semifinals of the Confederations Cup. With four points from their first two matches, the Socceroos were in a very strong position. They could even afford to lose their final group match against the host nation. Which was just as well. The Saudis finished 1–0 winners, and Venables finally suffered his first loss in charge of Australia. The coach said afterwards he had been thrilled and delighted with his unbeaten record. 'But it had to end sometime,' he added. And there were mitigating circumstances.

News of the industrial action had leaked the day before the match. In many ways, the players had their minds elsewhere. They also knew they could, in all probability, afford to lose to the Saudis; it was what Soccer Australia could afford which concerned them. A place in the semifinals would yield an extra $800 000 in prizemoney. When the squad members heard and read of Soccer Australia's public response to the stand-off, they were even more determined to force the issue. While a chastened Hill, by now at odds with the team, refused to comment, a spokesman for the federation jumped into the debate to accuse the players of 'sabre-rattling'. 'Is their conduct reasonable? No,' said the spokesman. 'The problem appears to be that the players stood to make a lot of money if we had made the World Cup finals. Obviously they're upset about missing out on really big earnings. But at a time when Australia is looking to these players to restore confidence and faith, their action reflects very poorly on them. Putting a gun to our head doesn't make the money appear.'

Winning games, however, does. And the Socceroos had won a lot more than they had lost. When Brazil went on to edge out Mexico 3–2 in the later match of the double-header, Australia were through to the semifinals despite the loss to Saudi Arabia. The pot of gold grew bigger. The stake for the players went up to $22 000 per man, but this still only represented less than a quarter of the total. The players felt a 50/50 split—common in many other countries—was a more reasonable policy. And while they would continue to play under protest, their dissatisfaction was clear. Venables maintained he had nothing to do with the crisis, but when asked if it made for an unhappy camp, he sagely replied, 'It doesn't help.'

By the time the Socceroos met Uruguay in the semifinal two days later, Hill was back in Sydney. He had left with a clear ultimatum from the squad: the matter would not be finalised until agreement was reached with the players' union. In the interim, the union reserved the right to withdraw its labour for the four nations tournament due to be played in Australia seven weeks later. The good news was that the flashpoint had passed, and now the team—and the nation—could finally focus on the task at hand.

Like the Socceroos, Uruguay had failed to qualify for the World Cup, but they were worthy opposition nonetheless. New coach Victor Pua had opted to bring a squad of young players to Riyadh, with the next Olympic Games (under-23) campaign in mind. The backbone of the squad came from the impressive under-20 team which had finished runners-up in the World Youth Championships six months earlier. In players like Marcelo Zalayeta, Alvaro Recoba and Nicolas Olivera, the Uruguayans possessed exceptional young talent. All three had their chances against an Australian XI that contained four changes to the team that had succumbed to the Saudis. But again Bosnich was in inspired form, and again a defence marshalled superbly by Ivanovic held firm. It was an ugly game. It was a war of attrition. It was probably a game Uruguay deserved to win. But they didn't. The final whistle went, and still there were no goals. But two minutes into extra time, it was over. Kewell, restored to the side, ended the contest with a thumping left-foot drive. A golden goal. Australia had triumphed 1–0 to reach their first-ever FIFA final.

The Socceroos had made history. Exactly three weeks after the lowest of lows, they had scaled the greatest of heights. Whatever would transpire in the final against Brazil, they had covered themselves in glory. FIFA named Zelic, Bosnich and Foster in a preliminary list of 33 players for a tournament all-star XI. Zelic ultimately made the final cut. The Socceroos were being recognised among the best in the world. But the very best remained Brazil.

D/E/S/E/R/T S/T/O/R/M

The history books will judge the final harshly. A week after restricting the world's best team to a scoreless draw, the Socceroos were thrashed 6–0—their nemesis Romario grabbing a hat-trick, as did Ronaldo. It was Australia's worst defeat for 42 years, and the third worst in history. But if the result was a painful reminder of how far the Socceroos had to go to be regarded among the true elite of the game, there had been some excuses. Viduka was sent off midway through the first half for a reckless challenge on Cafu, and with him went any chance of Australia keeping the scoreline to respectable proportions. Brazil, too, were motivated for revenge. The cheek of the Socceroos in holding them to a scoreless draw was fresh in their minds. They badly wanted to put the Australians in their place. They did, but it needs to be said that Brazil would have beaten any team in the world on this display. Even by Brazil's high standards, they possessed an exceptional team. And this was an exceptional performance. There was no disgrace in losing—albeit comprehensively—to a team in such irresistable form.

And so four days before Christmas the year had finally come to an end. It was a year that had begun on a high note and ended on an even higher one. But what really mattered—getting to the World Cup—had been lost in between. For the younger generation, there would be the chance to make amends, but for Arnold, Ivanovic and Slater there would be no reprieve. And for the likes of Aurelio Vidmar, Tobin, Hooker, Tapai and Trimboli, the chances of still being around in 2001 seemed increasingly remote. All these players had cut their teeth as part-timers in the national league, and had all learned to appreciate the true meaning of success. They knew that the chance of a lifetime had slipped through their fingers. They knew it was never meant to be. And they all hoped the Socceroos, and all that they stood for, would have better luck next time. It was time to turn the page for the next generation.

CHAPTER 14

THE FAB FIVE

IF THE FUTURE FOR THE SOCCEROOS REMAINS a collective responsibility, it is also about individuals. And if there is some solace to be gained from the agony of the World Cup demise, it is that Australia now possesses some of the finest players in its history. While the next World Cup attempt seems a long way off, it remains within the reach of the 'X' generation—those players who by the new millennium should be either at their peak or just about there.

The 1997 campaign signalled the end, or at least the beginning of the end, of several significant careers—not least Graham Arnold and Robbie Slater, regulars in the national squad for a decade. For Alex Tobin, Aurelio Vidmar, Ernie Tapai and Robbie Hooker, among others, the time to bid farewell to the green and gold is within sight. Yet if a new chapter is upon us, it is not without hope, or ambition. The ability of Australian soccer to keep producing players of international quality will ultimately yield its due reward. And if France 98 will be a sore point for years to come, it may not be too long before the Socceroos can atone.

The first World Cup of the next century will be historic in many ways—the first to be held in Asia, and the first to be shared between two countries (South Korea and Japan). Australia has every reason to believe it can also share in the sense of occasion, for the next backbone of the national team will arguably be the strongest ever. Some of these players are survivors of the 1992 Olympic (under-23) team, which remains the best Australia has ever produced. Ned Zelic, Paul Okon and Mark Bosnich will be the leaders of the 2001 campaign, and they should be at their peak. Harry Kewell came from nowhere to star in the climactic stages of the 1997 campaign, and could be followed by stylish defender Hayden Foxe, whose talent has only been glimpsed because of a dreadful run of injuries.

Others could emerge in much the same way, the Sydney 2000 Olympic team providing the perfect breeding ground for a new generation of Socceroos. But if there are many imponderables, there remains a group of players which, circumstances permitting, should help the Socceroos do what they have failed to do since 1974—qualify for the World Cup. They are the class of the new millennium.

THE GOALKEEPER
MARK BOSNICH

Flamboyant is a description that sits easily with Mark Bosnich, arguably Australia's most famous player. For he is a larger than life character, just as comfortable discussing the Koran as the merits of a 4-4-2 compared with a 5-3-2. A man with a liking for fat cigars, stretch limousines and expensive champagne, he is also blessed with a common touch—equally at home in the company of millionaire directors as he is with the tattooed army behind the goal he guards at Aston Villa's delightful home ground.

But if he has long been regarded as one of the best goalkeepers in the world, there have been recurring question marks about his character. Eccentricity may be worn as a badge of honour among keepers, but there are times when a steady head, and hands, are required. Bosnich's career has been littered with moments of recklessness. If there was one player, though, who proved a point in the white heat of the World Cup play-offs against Iran, it was the Socceroo no. 1. In Tehran, especially, Bosnich came of age—as a player, and as a man. His position as the first-choice keeper for the national team now seems secure for years to come. Bosnich will be 29 in the next World Cup campaign and, providing his form and fitness remains, could well play in two more World Cups after that. Given the somewhat chequered start to his Socceroo career, it says much about his growing maturity that he could leave the international stage as Australia's most capped and most successful player. Bosnich has now sorted out just where the national team sits in his list of priorities, and the good news for Australia is that playing in the World Cup finals has become his no. 1 goal in the game.

Having come close in both 1993 and 1997, he remains confident his ambition will be realised. And if the Socceroos do qualify for the 2002 tournament in Japan and South Korea, then expect Bosnich to confirm his pedigree. He is a player who thrives under pressure, and one who would savour the opportunity to be compared with the best in the world. Although he has been playing regularly in England's Premier League since 1993, he appreciates that only the World Cup can offer the appropriate stage for comparison. Bosnich is driven to realise his ambition, for perhaps the only fear he has is not to realise his potential.

That potential was evident at the age of 16, when he flew to England to trial with the two biggest clubs in the country, Manchester United and Liverpool, and had the choice of either. He opted for the former, and spent three eventful years at Old Trafford, working his way to the fringe of the first team before a work permit problem forced him to beat a hasty retreat to Australia. It was likely to be only a temporary sojourn, and when he married his English girlfriend he had the entree back into the big time. But although Manchester United wanted him back, he chose Aston Villa instead, confident that his passage to the first team would be easier at Villa Park than at Old Trafford, where the imposing Peter Schmeichel blocked his way. It was the right decision, and after a couple of seasons battling for his place he has become a fixture in the top side at Aston Villa, doing well enough to be voted among the top five keepers in the league.

His parallel career with the national team began less smoothly. He retired from the Socceroos in 1993 when coach Eddie Thomson demanded he show up for the World Cup match in Canada rather than stay in England to fight for his spot with Aston Villa. It was a short-lived sabbatical, and Bosnich returned to the fold in time for the ensuing play-offs against Argentina. But his appearances for the Socceroos remained frustratingly infrequent between the 1993 and 1997 World Cup campaigns—he had been capped just five times when Terry Venables assumed control.

But Bosnich was reinvigorated by Venables' arrival, and discovered to his liking that playing for Australia was something he had missed a lot more than he had realised. He liked it even more when he became the first goalkeeper ever to score for his country, adding the final goal in a 13–0 World Cup drubbing of the Solomon Islands from the penalty spot after he ran the length of the field to demand the ball from a teammate. It was typical Bosnich showmanship, but it was also typical that his shot never looked like missing.

His years in the Premier League have taught him that accepting responsibility is not to be done lightly. Never was this more evident that in Tehran, when Bosnich produced three world-class saves in daunting circumstances to deny Iran the victory they probably deserved. Rather than be intimidated by the 128 000 screaming fans, he relished the atmosphere. Bosnich is a player for the big occasion, his best performances often reserved for the biggest stage. Positionally, he is exceptional. Physically, he is imposing. And athletically, he is outstanding. Until Tehran, only his temperament had sometimes let him down.

A penchant for generating the wrong kind of headlines may have cost him dearly, and he admits he can never guarantee he won't make the same mistakes again. But Bosnich is always willing to learn.

THE SWEEPER
PAUL OKON

Paul Okon had one hope of salvaging a demoralising year in 1997: the decisive World Cup qualifier against Iran at the Melbourne Cricket Ground. It had been circled in his diary for months; it was the target, the salvation, of a year virtually destroyed by yet another knee injury. Okon did everything in his power to meet the deadline. For the first leg in Tehran, he was content to bide his time and nurse his knee through a light training regime in order to be available for the return leg at the MCG. When the team flew back to Melbourne, Okon went on to Sydney for a final consultation with his specialists. Much to his delight, he was given the all-clear and when he rejoined the squad the following day he was ready to put himself through full-scale training for the first time in eight months.

The public, and the media, waited with bated breath to see if the country's oustanding player would finally make his long-awaited comeback in the green and gold. For two days the Okon story dominated the headlines. Terry Venables fuelled the speculation by declining to commit himself. In the meantime, Okon pushed himself hard, and although his knee remained sore he had no doubt he was ready to play a role. At the very least, he was certain he was up to a place on the substitute's bench. But the afternoon before the match, Okon received the news he had been dreading. He was not to be involved at all.

Who knows what difference Okon could have made on that fateful evening. But there is a fair case that a player who can play either as sweeper or defensive midfield would have steadied the ship during the decisive four-minute spell which cost the Socceroos a berth at the World Cup. Venables' curious reluctance to gamble on Okon, even as a reserve, remains a mystery. It was a non-selection that could well have cost the Socceroos dearly.

It was not as if Venables was unaware of Okon's ability. Four weeks earlier, he had made a special trip to Rome to watch him in a reserve team match for Lazio—a performance which only fortified his belief that he was a special talent indeed. It was something others had known for years. From the moment he'd forced his way into the Marconi-Fairfield first team at the age of 17, Okon had stamped himself as a player of great maturity. Skillful, quick, and composed, he was the perfect *libero*—able to read the play superbly and bring the ball out of defence with ease. So good was he in this position that he ultimately forced his peer and great rival Ned Zelic to move into midfield. But Zelic and Okon had something else in common—their susceptibility to injury—and it has cost the former heavily in terms of his international career. After the Melbourne match, Okon lamented, 'I've been involved in two World Cups but I've only played five times for my country, and that hurts.'

Certainly Okon's future in the green and gold should be far better than his past. After all, this is the player nominated by none other than the legendary Franz Beckenbauer as one of the best *libero*s he had seen, the player voted Belgian Player of the Year in 1995, and the Oceania Footballer of the Year 12 months later; the player who opened the door to his hotel room in Brussels, and found Italy's most decorated footballer, Dino Zoff, standing there and asking if he would like to join Lazio in a deal which would make him a multimillionaire overnight. Okon is world-class, arguably the only Australian with a genuine claim to the title, and the enduring frustration has been that his countrymen have rarely had the pleasure of seeing his talents first-hand.

On a rare domestic outing for the Socceroos, against Ghana in a friendly international in Sydney, Okon showed Australian fans just what all the fuss was about. His display that afternoon ranks as one of the most dominant ever produced by a Socceroo, and there was every reason to believe he would play a crucial role in guiding the national team into France 98. But as he struggled with knee and groin problems in the first half of his first season in Italy's *Serie A*, he began to fear the worst. And, sure enough, just as he was looking forward to the World Cup campaign, he broke down. There would be no miracle, and when the year ended Okon remained the only first-choice player still to play under Venables.

It might have been a different story, perhaps, if the coach had gambled at the MCG. The storyline may even have had a happy ending. Okon, certainly, remains disappointed that he was not called upon in Australia's hour of need. But his time should come next time around, when he should be at his peak. As a *libero*, Okon has two more World Cups left in him. And for a player who is pained by the infrequency of his Socceroo appearances, 2001 cannot arrive quickly enough.

For those desperate to see him blossom on the international stage, there is also a sense of urgency. In 1993, he was a young player on the outside looking in, and was given just one outing in the match away to Canada. In 1997, he was ready to make his mark, only to be cut down by injury. In 2001, providing his fitness has returned, he could well provide the difference between success and failure as the Socceroos strive to end their World Cup misery. Okon is that influential, and that good.

THE DEFENDER
HAYDEN FOXE

Hayden Foxe was the invisible man of the Atlanta Olympics, which goes some way to explaining his low profile in his own country. But if the nation has yet to learn of the exceptional talents of the tall, athletic, elegant defender, then the hope is that his star will be in the ascendancy before too long.

If Foxe epitomises the new generation of Australian talent, then one quality sets him apart: an old-fashioned passion for the green and gold shirt. 'I'd do anything to play for Australia; it's just the way I am,' he says. Combine that fierce devotion to the Socceroos with his outstanding ability, and Foxe seems destined to figure prominently in the next World Cup campaign.

By then he will be 24—still relatively young, but having learnt from his experiences at both club and international level. The education process has not been easy—his career has already been hampered by serious injury—but with each setback he has emerged as a stronger and more determined individual. Mark him down not only as a future regular with the national team, but also as a potential Socceroo captain. Foxe is a leader in every sense of the word. Raised in Sydney's western suburbs, where he spent his junior football with the well-organised Blacktown City club, Foxe first stepped into the international arena with the Australian under-17 team. By that stage he was ensconced at the AIS in Canberra, where he alternated between midfield and defence as the coaching staff encouraged him to work on all sides of his game. In his final season at the AIS in 1994–95, he was a convincing winner of the national youth league Player of the Year award, and even at the tender age of 17 was obviously a player of huge potential.

Foxe never made the move into the national league, preferring instead to opt for the direct route to Europe. And he could hardly have chosen a better platform to continue his education—Ajax Amsterdam are widely regarded as having the best youth system of any club in the world. Although registered as an amateur, Foxe was afforded all the privileges of the professionals—and this at a time when Ajax were club champions of Europe and boasted arguably the best crop of players in their history. A regular in the reserve team at Ajax, Foxe spent much of the season playing alongside exceptional players, among them Brazilian World Cup winner Marcio Santos and emerging Nigerian star Nwanko Kanu. It was an eye-opening environment for the young Australian, but he never looked out of place. In his typically laconic style, Foxe refused to be overawed by his surroundings. It was a surprise, therefore, that Ajax failed to offer him a decent contract to turn professional. His potential was clear to see.

Foxe could have stayed in Holland—both FC Utrecht and NAC Breda were keen to sign him—but instead he returned home to answer the call of his country, making his debut for the Olympic (under-23) team in the final play-offs against Canada. Foxe was prominent in both legs, making a dreadful mistake to help the Canadians scores in Edmonton, but hitting the target at the right end in Sydney as the Olyroos booked their passage to the Atlanta Olympics. His career, and his reputation, looked set to take off.

Sadly, however, injury intervened. Foxe went to the Olympics of 1996 but returned home as the only player not to have set foot on the park. A niggling ankle injury put paid to his Olympic dream. But the experience was not a total disaster; a sportsman who proclaims himself a proud Australian remained behind to cheer on his countrymen at other sports—yelling himself hoarse as the women's hockey team won gold. Foxe knew then, as if there were any doubt, that his primary duty was to his country. But he would have to wait for his chance.

An operation to fix his ankle effectively sidelined him for a season, but his rehabilitation at the AIS was good enough to convince German club Arminia Bielefeld that he was worth investing in for the future. Foxe finally made his long-awaited comeback midway through 1997—not with his new club, but again in Australian colours. He was a key player for the national under-20 team at the World Youth Championships in Malaysia.

Following the championships, Foxe flew on to Germany, but again fate was to deal a cruel blow. This time it was a foot injury which slowed his progress, and although he struggled manfully against the odds—even making his Bundesliga debut off the bench—it was a losing battle. Again injury had cursed him, reducing him to a virtual spectator's role in his debut season at Bielefeld.

But he did retain an interest in the progress of the Socceroos under Venables, and for special reason. Two of his clubmates, Ali Daei and Karim Bagheri, figured prominently in Australia's ultimate demise. The Iranian duo were quick to remind Foxe of the fact when they returned in triumph to Germany.

'Let's just say I was still dirty about what had happened, and I let them know it,' he says.

The desire to make amends now burns deeply in Foxe, who has made the 2001 World Cup campaign a priority. Before then he is likely to star at the Sydney 2000 Olympics, but he has been around football long enough to know that the World Cup remains the real thing. Although he prefers to play as sweeper, Foxe accepts that his promotion into the Socceroo ranks could well come as a marker. 'I'm not big on the position, but if it means getting a guernsey with the Socceroos, then I'll be happy to play anywhere,' he says.

The sweeper's position could well come Foxe's way eventually, but in the interim he has all the attributes to become a dominant force in the Socceroos rearguard. 'I guess my best asset is that I don't panic, no matter what the situation,' Foxe says. 'I like to play my way out of trouble—there's no way I'm going to kick and run.'

THE PLAYMAKER
NED ZELIC

If there has been one consistency in Ned Zelic's turbulent career, it has been his inconsistency. The weight of expectation which has followed him ever since his wonder goal gained Australia a place in the 1992 Barcelona Olympics has burdened his soul, and his outlook.

Zelic has long believed he has been the victim of inflated demands. 'Every time I get the ball people seem to think I should go on a run, beat four or five players, and set up a goal,' he once said. 'It doesn't work like that.'

True enough. But like all players blessed with a touch of genius, Zelic must learn to live with the pressure of high expectation. There are no hiding places on the pitch for those who can open up the play. And if that is something Zelic has struggled to deal with more often than not, there was enough evidence during the failed 1997 World Cup assault to suggest he has begun to win his battle with the demons within.

From the first qualifier against the Solomon Islands to the decisive match against Iran, Zelic was the Socceroos' most consistent performer. Others may have had better spells and better games, but the thread running throughout the campaign was Zelic's measured contribution from midfield: full of purpose, full of poise, occasional flashes of sublime skill, plenty of running and a couple of well-taken goals during the Oceania rounds.

For a player who has had plenty of ups and downs, it was a delight to see Zelic so… well… reliable. Venables made him an ever-present, and the player rewarded him for his faith. This was the coming of age of Australia's next Big Thing. A little late, perhaps, but immensely pleasing nonetheless.

In 2001, when the Socceroos next attempt to make the World Cup, Zelic should be in his prime. At 30 years of age his legs may have slowed, but his vision should be razor sharp. And Zelic's best attribute has always been his ability to see the options that others can't. He may have made his name initially as a sweeper, and he may even return to that position before he retires, but in the interim his skills can be best utilised as a playmaker, and it is in the centre of the park that he is again likely to figure in the quest for the World Cup of 2002.

That there is now a sense of destiny about his Socceroo future speaks volumes for the way in which he has emerged from arguably the darkest period of his career. Zelic went into the 1997 campaign having barely kicked a ball at club level for three years. But it didn't show. He thrived under the responsibility placed upon him by Venables, and the rest of the dressing-room noticed how much more relaxed he seemed. The introverted, somewhat suspicious character of the years before had been replaced by a more jovial, humble person. Married just before the Oceania qualifiers, the new-found stability in his private life was reflected both on and off the park.

That stability, however, continued to be absent from his club career, where Zelic had developed an unenviable reputation as a player who was difficult to control. Eight clubs in his first seven years of senior football suggested the obvious—that Zelic found it hard to stay in one place. And virtually every transfer had been dogged by controversy, right from the beginning when he moved from Sydney United to Sydney Olympic—after he had posed for photographs in a Marconi-Fairfield strip.

THE FAB FIVE

Perhaps Zelic's best period of his career was his spell at Borussia Dortmund, where he enjoyed a memorable first season with one of Germany's strongest clubs before injury and self-doubt eroded his confidence. A subsequent move to England and Queens Park Rangers proved disastrous, and Zelic even began publicly to contemplate whether he had the mental strength to persevere with his football career. After a short loan spell back in Germany with Eintracht Frankfurt, he thought he had turned the corner with a move to French champions Auxerre, but a falling out with manager Guy Roux soon consigned him to a permanent role in the reserves. It was at this time that he was rescued by the World Cup campaign, and his form for the Socceroos indicated he was finally ready to emerge from three seasons of personal hell. Another move on loan back to Germany, this time to 1860 Munich, followed the World Cup campaign, and the hope is that Zelic will be able to build on his rejuvenation at international level by reinvigorating his club career. Certainly Germany is where he seems most appreciated and most content. His coach at Borussia Dortmund, Ottmar Hitzfeld, remarked to Zelic's Socceroo teammate Robbie Slater at the 1998 Oceania Footballer of the Year dinner in Munich that Zelic should never have left the Westfalenstadion. He may have had a point.

But as Zelic looks forward to the prime years of his career, the feeling is that he is finally ready to shed his chequered past and stabilise his future. More mature as a player, and as a person, he seems determined to make up for lost time. Twice named in FIFA World XI teams, there has never been any doubt about his ability. Those who recall his masterful display as a 19-year-old rookie for the Socceroos, when he dominated an England attack which included Gary Lineker, recognised a rare talent. But until the 1997 World Cup campaign, six years later, that talent had been displayed only in patches. Too often, perhaps, Zelic felt others were to blame. But now he has recognised the onus is on his own shoulders. Physically, he looks to have recovered from his succession of knee operations. Mentally, he looks fresh and motivated. There is every reason to believe that the 2001 World Cup campaign will provide the platform for Zelic to crown his career.

THE STRIKER
HARRY KEWELL

When Harry Kewell was an adolescent hopeful, he used to follow the skills contests around the various shopping centres of western Sydney, picking up more than his share of prizes in the process. Steve Darby, in those days development officer for Soccer Australia, recalls a scrawny, somewhat shy youth whose demeanour grew markedly more confident when the ball was at his feet. And in what seemed to be the blink of an eye, all that precocious enthusiasm was suddenly manifesting itself on two of the biggest stages possible—the English Premier League and the World Cup. Harry Kewell emerged to become *the* story of the Socceroos' final hurdle in their quest to qualify for France 98.

Harry, Harry, Harry Kewell, he's so cool, Harry Kewell, sang the crowd at the MCG on the night that Australia's hopes died a painful death against Iran. And the youngest member of the team did not disappoint. Kewell struck sweetly to score the Socceroos' opening goal, to follow his goal a week earlier in Tehran. All of a sudden, within the space of a few months, Kewell had arrived in the big time. But for those who had chartered his early career there was no element of surprise. Rarely had his coaches at the New South Wales Academy, David Lee and Oscar Gonzalez, dealt with a youngster so obsessed by his football. 'To be honest, I don't think he was interested in schoolwork all that much,' Gonzalez recalls.

The hard work obviously paid off. As a member of the Australian under-17 team which travelled to the world championships in Ecuador in 1995, he had impressed as a left-sided player. And it was in this position that the Socceroo coach, Eddie Thomson, gave him his senior debut against Chile less than a year later. By that time Kewell had flown the coop and joined Leeds, his offer of a contract supported by that fact that unlike the other Australian triallist who went with him to England, Brett Emerton, he was lucky enough to have a British passport. Kewell, whose father had emigrated from London, immediately felt right at home at Elland Road.

It didn't take him long to make an impression. In his first season at the club, manager Howard Wilkinson handed him his first team debut towards the end of the season, when nothing was at stake and the coaching staff felt ready to blood some of the club's crop of outstanding youngsters. But the following season started off badly for Leeds, and when Wilkinson was sacked to make way for George Graham, a results-first policy meant the youngsters would have to bide their time.

THE FAB FIVE

Yet while Graham concentrated on the expediency of fighting off relegation, he remained well aware of Kewell's potential. By the time the 1996–97 season kicked off, that potential could no longer be ignored.

Graham, a close friend of Venables since their playing days together at Chelsea three decades earlier, provided a succession of gentle reminders to the Socceroo coach that his young Australian might be worth a look at. Venables, however, resisted the temptation for the Oceania stages of the World Cup campaign, preferring to allow Kewell the time to develop his club career. But finally, when Paul Okon again succumbed to injury for the friendly in Tunisia—the final warm-up match for the play-offs against Iran—Venables decided it was time to act.

Kewell was a late addition to the squad, and came off the bench in the second half to impress in his now-favoured position as striker. When he returned to Elland Road from Tunis and weighed in with a couple of well-struck goals for Leeds, the clamour for his inclusion in the World Cup squad gained momentum. Venables also sensed the time was right, and the rest is history. Kewell won the battle to win the second striking role alongside Mark Viduka, and scored in both legs against Iran to cement his reputation as Australia's outstanding up-and-comer. At the age of 19, he had shown that nothing was beyond him. There was a refreshing audacity about his play.

A few weeks later, Kewell was again in on the act to score the deciding goal in the semifinals of the Confederations Cup, sending the Socceroos into the final at Uruguay's expense. In the final against Brazil, he fashioned Australia's only real opening of the match. His rich vein of form dovetailed nicely with the saturation coverage he had received since his selection for the World Cup play-offs. Within a matter of weeks, Kewell was able to stamp himself as Australian soccer's most promotable star—all without saying very much on his own behalf. Young, talented and handsome, he possessed all the ingredients to excite the interest of mainstream Australia, even if he remained a man of few words. Because, above all, he was good—very good indeed.

By the time the next World Cup campaign arrives, Kewell is likely to have had five tough years of professional football behind him. Graham has made it a priority to hold on to one of the club's prized assets. Kewell should also have featured in the Sydney 2000 Olympics, as well as most of the Socceroos' most important matches, before the 2001 campaign.

What it should add up to is a striker who may finally be able to provide the national team with a worthy successor to the last player to score regularly for the

Socceroos—John Kosmina. And most significantly, Kewell has enough self-belief and will to win to fulfil his enormous promise.

'The best thing about Harry is that he gets better if his team is behind,' says his former New South Wales Academy coach, David Lee. 'He seems to be able to find another gear.' That extra gear makes Kewell the right kind of player to lead the Socceroos at the sharp end of the park. A scorer, a fighter, and a winner—the perfect combination for what lies ahead. Kewell is not the sort of personality who will allow his career to end without the opportunity of playing in the World Cup.

CHAPTER 15

BACK TO BASICS

WHAT A DIFFERENCE A YEAR MAKES. When Venables first arrived in Australia to take up his duties as Socceroo coach, the atmosphere surrounding the four nations tournament was one of unbridled optimism and eager anticipation. It was the beginning of an exciting adventure, one that would hopefully lead to a place in France 98. But when Venables returned for the second edition of the same event 12 months later, the World Cup dream was over, and mood was one of almost complete indifference. Apathy reigned. There was even a time when it seemed the series might not go ahead—until the sponsors, Optus World, reminded Soccer Australia of their contractual obligations.

Those obligations were met, and eventually the national body announced the identity of the three visiting teams who would provide the Australian public with their first chance to see the Socceroos since the unforgettable night at the MCG. Chile, Japan and South Korea had agreed to play a home-based Australian team, although there was a notable difference in format. The inaugural event had been a tournament, with all the teams playing each other in a series of double-headers. This time, however, the touring sides would only be playing one-off internationals against Australia. Chile had to rush off and play England at Wembley just four days after the match in Melbourne. Japan and South Korea were in a position to hang around after playing the Socceroos, but they had to be content with playing club sides rather than against each other. They didn't mind. If the atmosphere surrounding the Socceroo squad was one of post–World Cup depression, the three visiting teams offered a stark contrast. They were bubbling with enthusiasm, for a very good reason. Unlike the Socceroos, Chile, Japan and South Korea were on their way to the World Cup. The trip to Australia marked the beginning of the final countdown. Their opponents could only look on in envy.

In that context, the question most asked was what point the games would be serving. Although he never said as much, the impression was that Venables—fresh from his tribulations at Portsmouth—had his mind on other matters. Some of the survivors of an emotionally draining World Cup campaign also admitted privately they were struggling to get motivated.

As it happened, the focus was not so much on the games but rather on conjecture over Venables' future. Six weeks earlier, Hill had sanctioned a press release from Saudi Arabia stating that Venables had agreed in principle to stay on. In truth, he had jumped the gun. Venables may have agreed to the concept of continuing with the Socceroos, but he had not agreed to anything of substance. And on several occasions in his newspaper column over the ensuing weeks he was to refer to his time with Australia in the past tense.

There was certainly a growing restlessness within the soccer community to see the situation resolved. Many saw the argument as a simple one—if Venables was to remain on a long-term basis, he had to move to Australia. If he didn't wish to leave London, his time with the Socceroos was up. In typically forthright fashion, former Socceroo coach Frank Arok gave voice to those sentiments:

'We can no longer afford to have a visiting professor. He [Venables] was good for public relations, but we do not need an adviser. We need a creator with vision, and in that respect he failed completely. If he was prepared to move here, then it could be different. He could get the feel for the players, and for the game here, instead of being led by somebody else. At the moment, it's like the blind leading the blind.'

When the Socceroo squad was announced via the now-familiar video conference from a television studio in London, Venables was unable to shed any more light on his future. All he could say was that he was still waiting on a firm offer from Soccer Australia. He suggested that the basis for a new contract might be presented during his impending visit to Australia.

Hill insisted there was no urgency given that Venables still had six months of his existing contract to run. Nonetheless, the clear signal from the coach was that he could not ignore alternative offers of employment for too much longer. Glasgow

BACK TO BASICS

Rangers, Liverpool, Everton, Real Madrid—take your pick. The message being that Venables was priming himself to return to big-time club football in Europe. Hill seemed to be fighting a lost cause. Not that he ever saw it that way.

Venables finally arrived in Sydney at the end of January and immediately locked himself away in his apartment at The Rocks to try and thrash out a deal with his employers. Yet when he emerged to face the media in a hastily arranged press conference six days later, nothing of significance had been resolved. 'We are not in a position to offer Terry Venables a detailed proposal,' admitted Hill. Part of the reason was financial—Soccer Australia's bank balance had taken a battering from an expensive World Cup campaign and there was nothing left in the kitty.

Money apart, Venables also wanted assurances that the Socceroos would, in future, be involved more often in meaningful international competitions. He did not want to sign a new deal only to spend the next three years being fed a diet of low-key friendly games. Soccer Australia could provide no such guarantees.

'Yes, he [Hill] wants me to stay but he hasn't actually given me anything to think about because he hasn't got it—he hasn't got any games,' Venables proclaimed.

As a result of the impasse, speculation continued unabated. Throughout the Optus World series Venables was forced to continually field questions on his future. Nobody seemed too interested in the actual games. The task of promoting the series—already difficult enough in the post–World Cup period—developed into the ultimate 'hard sell'.

On the field, some hard decisions had already been made. Philosophically, there was a strong argument that having failed to get to the World Cup, this was the right occasion to give new blood the opportunity to impress. Former Socceroo skipper John Warren led the charge. He maintained that with the Olympic (under-23) team due to play against the touring Brazilians shortly afterwards, the timing was perfect to promote several of the Olyroos into the senior team. Whatever the case, Warren argued, the Socceroo squad should be picked with the next World Cup campaign in mind.

But those views were effectively ignored. When the squad was announced only two Olyroos, Brett Emerton and Bill Damianos, were on the list. And many of the 'newcomers' were, in fact, players who had been resurrected. The prospect of Abbas Saad, John Markovski, Dominic Longo and Fausto de Amicis being around for the 2001 campaign seemed highly unlikely.

It was difficult to identify a clear purpose to the selection. It was not a young squad. It was not a developmental squad. It was, simply, a squad purpose-built for the series without the long term in mind. Yet in that case, how could the glaring omission of striker Damian Mori be reconciled? Mori had been an ever-present during the World Cup campaign, and that was when the overseas-based players were available. Yet here he was, in the midst of a rich vein of scoring form for his club, Adelaide City, and he couldn't even make the stand-by list.

So it was with some confusion that the Socceroo players gathered in Melbourne to prepare for the opening game of the series against Chile. Why are we here? What do these games mean? Is Terry going to stay or go? On the last question, Venables could offer no further insights. All he could say was that he hoped to have something to consider before he returned to England after the series was completed.

In other circles, the attention began to focus on who might be his successor, it was a question Soccer Australia was not inclined to seriously address. Instead, every effort was being put into producing a package to keep Venables involved. Among the options being canvassed was the offer of a role with the Olyroos in the lead-up to Sydney 2000, and perhaps the addition of a director of coaching job to his repertoire. Concerted efforts would also be made to get the Socceroos invited, on a regular basis, to the Asian Championships. And then there was the question of money. Venables didn't come cheap. The truth was Soccer Australia didn't have the funds to pay him in the manner to which he had become accustomed. And so approaches were made to the private sector in the hope that some generous business interests might be inclined to help out.

Yet if the hierarchy of Soccer Australia couldn't bear the thought of life without Venables, others could. A strong lobby emerged to suggest that if he wasn't prepared to move to Australia, his loss might not be such a disaster. Certainly several key areas which had previously been the responsibility of the national coach—among them coaching other coaches, helping the youth teams and working with the AIS— had been neglected during Venables' 12 months in charge.

Momentum began to build for someone who might be able to take a more holistic approach; perhaps even an Australian-born coach, something the Socceroos had never had. Indeed, while Venables was taking his squad through their paces in Melbourne, some of the best local candidates were completing an advanced coaching course in Canberra. Venables had been invited to attend the gathering at the AIS, but had declined. Again those local coaches who hoped to benefit from his experience were to be kept at arm's length. But Soccer Australia, largely urged on by the efforts of board member George Negus, was beginning to seriously consider a long-awaited change in policy. Local coaches—among them Angie Postecoglou and Nick

BACK TO BASICS

Theodorakopoulos—had started to work under Raul Blanco with the Olyroo team. More were promised the opportunity to sample life at international level. After so many years of being ignored, at least it was a start.

The Socceroos started the Optus World series in less than convincing fashion. On a drenching night in Melbourne they lost for the first time at home under Venables. Chile may have been without their two star forwards, Marcelo Salas and Ivan Zamorano, but they were clearly the better team in front of a 12 000 crowd dominated by their own boisterous supporters. The only goal of the game arrived midway through the first half, at a stage when Chile were in complete control of proceedings. After a telling pass for Jose Luis Sierra the Socceroos were, once again, caught square at the back. A stronger second half showing at least gave Venables some heart, and of the four debutantes, playmaker Troy Halpin stood out. After coming off the bench at half-time, the intelligent schemer immediately picked up the pace of the game, and his close control comfortably matched the quality of his South American opponents. It was a meteoric rise for Halpin, who only a month earlier was warming the bench for his hometown club, Newcastle Breakers. After making it clear he wanted to leave a struggling side to further his international ambitions, Halpin transferred to Perth Glory and was immediately rewarded with his first Socceroo call-up.

The second cap came four days later, and this time Halpin was involved from the start. If Venables had been reluctant to experiment during the inaugural tournament 12 months before, he was now happy to give everyone a start. The pressure for results was off, and the intention was to test out the newcomers in his squad. Six changes were made for the second game of the series against South Korea in Sydney, and it worked. Like the Chileans, the visitors were below strength. But unlike the Chileans, Korea were blunt in front of goal. Most of their first-choice forward line and midfield was absent because of commitments with clubs in Japan or Europe. The Korean defence, however, was intact and was typically hard to breach. Yet in a breezy performance, highlighted by the sparkling display of Kris Trajanovski and strong efforts from Halpin, de Amicis and Saad, the Socceroos triumphed 1–0. The goal was brilliantly worked, and perfectly executed by Ernie Tapai, another player who impressed. Although several contentious refereeing decisions were hotly disputed by the Korean coach, Cha Bum-kun, nothing could detract from a marvellous Australian performance. They may be the best team in Asia, but South Korea historically have a hard time of it against the

Socceroos. And once again, they were to leave empty-handed. The only disappointing aspect of an encouraging evening was the size of the crowd. Barely 9000 fans showed up at the cavernous Sydney Football Stadium—confirming that the Socceroos had lost support in the aftermath of the World Cup demise.

Interest, at least, was higher for the final match of the series in Adelaide against Japan. Not only had the Japanese brought their full-strength squad, but the game marked the official opening of the refurbished Hindmarsh Stadium. There was one other point of intrigue—would this be Venables' final appearance in the Socceroo dugout? Ultimately, no conclusions were to be reached, but the game did mark one significant farewell: the ageless warrior, Milan Ivanovic, announced that he would be making his last appearance in the green and gold. At the age of 37, the Yugoslav-born defender—who had arrived in Adelaide nine years before suspecting that his career was on the way down—decided the moment was right. He would say goodbye before his hometown fans, and with the luxury of being able to choose the time and manner of his departure. It was typical of a player, and a man, of his class. Over seven years and 59 games for his adopted country, he had formed a formidable partnership with his clubmate Alex Tobin at the heart of the defence. In that time Ivanovic had overcome the challenges of the much younger Ned Zelic, Paul Okon and Steve Horvat to make the sweeper's role his own. Indeed, many believed that Venables' decision to ignore Ivanovic in favour of Horvat for the deciding match against Iran had cost Australia a place in the World Cup finals. Ivanovic did not want to buy into the argument, except to say he was disappointed at being overlooked. And now his international career was set to expire.

Unfortunately, he did not get the send-off he had been hoping for. The match was as good as over after just four minutes, when de Amicis was dismissed by rookie referee Mark Shield for handling the ball on the goal line. The Japanese converted the resulting penalty and, despite some fine efforts from Saad and Trajanovski, the Socceroos never looked likely to bridge the gap. Ultimately, Japan finished comfortable 3–0 winners. Ivanovic was even denied the chance to wring some applause from the crowd. Just as Venables was preparing to substitute him in time to walk off to a standing ovation, the referee blew for full-time. For once in his career, Ivanovic had not timed his run to perfection.

CHAPTER 16

ALL IS NOT LOST

IT IS A GREY MIDSUMMER AFTERNOON AT Parklea on the north-west outskirts of Sydney. The sun has stayed behind the clouds but the humidity remains overpowering. The shirt of national staff coach Les Scheinflug is clinging to his back. Out on the field, the sweat is dripping from every pore. A group of whippet-like teenagers, in black attire, are sprinting up and down the park, hoping to impress Scheinflug sufficiently in a trial game to win a spot in the Australian under-17 team. It is the first month of 1998, and the beginning of a new era. The cycle is turning once again.

Just five weeks earlier, the Socceroos had bowed out of the World Cup. At many levels, the game has still to emerge from its period of mourning. But for those brought together for a training camp at the headquarters of Soccer NSW, the past is academic. Only time will tell whether Iain Fyfe, or Joss van Strattan, or Matthew Milosevic, or any of the 30 young pretenders will be able to make the grade, but for the next generation, it's the future that counts.

Sitting halfway up the makeshift grandstand, Graham Arnold is inclined to agree. Arnold was on the pitch at the end of the demoralising match against Iran. It was his fourth World Cup campaign as a player, and it would be his last. There would be no fairytale ending, no swan song at the World Cup finals. It hurt at the time, and it is a hurt that will never go away. But on this early January evening Arnold wants to forget all that. A few days earlier, Soccer Australia announced that a new club, the Northern Spirit, would be admitted to the national league. Arnold, still active as a player, was appointed as the club's inaugural coach. Which explains his presence at Parklea. He is doing what a good coach should: casting an eye over the next generation of home-grown talent, looking into his crystal ball and hoping he will get it right, for himself and for his new club. And at the end of a lively match, he makes his move. Two players have caught his attention. He motions them to come over to the fence. A few minutes later, the Northern Spirit have added two promising 18-year-olds to the stable for their debut season in the league. It is debatable who is more excited. On the way home, the player turned coach babbles about the potential of his new recruits. 'What about the big fullback? Some left foot!' And all the time Arnold is thinking, this is the beginning not the end.

If Australian soccer is remarkable for one thing, it is its resilience. For decades it has been buffeted by one setback after another: endless squabbling among its own officials; a chronic shortage of funds; spectator violence, much of it caused by ethnic tensions; an under-achieving national team; the shameful neglect by the mainstream media. One step forward, two steps back. Yet through all this, the game has inched towards the ultimate goal—acceptance. And it will come, for no other reason, perhaps, than its players. The proverbial sleeping giant of Australian sport will finally awaken. And then everything else will have to move out of the way.

This is the hope that Arnold clings to. The sport has been good to him—a lucrative professional career overseas, a well-paid job as a full-time coach upon his return, a million-dollar mansion in Sydney's northern suburbs, a lifetime of memories packed into a few, short years—but the truth is, Arnold will never be truly satisfied until he sees the sport assume its rightful prominence in Australia. At Parklea, he admires the quality of the young players displayed before his expert eye, he notes how much techniques have improved since he was the same age, with the same ambitions. He appreciates how much more effort has gone into their coaching, and how much opportunity they now have. Soccer may still sit behind the likes of cricket, rugby league, Australian football and rugby union in spectator appeal, but in terms of a career option it is catching up fast.

The momentum seems inexorable. And not only at the sharp end, among the players of international quality. Behind them is a vast reservoir of 500 000 registered players—a quarter of them in New South Wales alone—pushing at the dam wall. This is the past, the present and the future all rolled into one. No other team sport can boast such a weight of numbers. No other sport appeals to so many people from so many backgrounds. But the real potential of Australian soccer has still to be unlocked. What is needed is the right key.

The Socceroos have always been regarded as the most likely catalyst, and this hasn't changed, despite the painful end to the 1997 World Cup campaign. The national team remains the best possible advertisement for Australian soccer. When the Socceroos are on a roll—like they were in 1974 (World Cup finals), or in 1985 (World Cup play-offs against Scotland), or in 1988 (Seoul Olympics), or in 1993 (World Cup play-offs against Argentina), or most recently at the tail end of 1997—the level of interest explodes. These are the fertile times for the game, when the media, the sponsors and the public come out of the woodwork to declare their allegiance. So many promises are made, so much expectation is raised. But then the setback comes and the momentum disappears. All it needs is a mistimed tackle, a bad pass, a goalkeeping mistake, a miscued clearance. Big matches often hinge on such moments. And too often the luck in the games that matter, the ones which would qualify the Socceroos for the World Cup, goes against the green and gold. The peddlers of influence retreat into their shells; Australian soccer goes into hibernation for another four years.

It is an all too familiar story, and the burning question is how to break the boom–bust cycle. With the Socceroos having failed to qualify for France 98—the sixth missed opportunity in a row—the solution is no easier to find. But at least Soccer Australia has finally begun to canvass the big issues in the hope that the game can be freed from its World Cup shackles. How to sustain interest over a period of time is the essential ingredient.

Both Hill and Venables endorse the view that having the Socceroos involved more regularly in meaningful international tournaments could be the circuit-breaker. 'Name me one other country in the top 100 which has to wait four years for the big games,' lamented Venables in the aftermath of the World Cup demise. 'We must get an invitation to something like the Asian Championships [held every two years]. I would think we have earned that right.'

Having a legitimate case is one thing, getting it across the line another. The push to have Australia integrated into Asia, where football has become a phenomenon, has taken many forms over many years. And whenever Australia has pushed too hard, the Asians have blocked the way. The truth is that the Asians don't want a strong, competitive team like the Socceroos challenging for their trophies. It would require direct intervention from FIFA to get Australia an invitation to Asia's showpiece tournament. But stranger things have happened. And if the

Socceroos do force their way through the door, then suddenly the international calendar assumes more substance. The World Cup, following by the Confederations Cup, followed by the Asian Championships—a nice symmetry, and enough incentive for a genuine level of interest to be maintained.

Yet if a busy, productive national team can provide the impetus, the Socceroos cannot do it on their own. What happens underneath is also crucially important. And here, perhaps, lies the most encouraging sign that despite the latest World Cup heartache the game is well poised to make serious inroads. Nothing excites Australians more than the Olympics and Sydney 2000 looms as the ideal stage for Australian soccer to rejuvenate its international image. For the short term, at least, it could well be the Olyroos, and not the Socceroos, who occupy centre stage.

Australia's performances at the last three Olympics have been encouraging. In 1988 in Seoul, when senior teams were involved, the Socceroos qualified for the quarterfinals after a famous victory in the group stage over Yugoslavia. Four years later, the eligibility rules were altered and the tournament was restricted to players under 23 years of age. It was a welcome change, and the quality of football at Barcelona in 1992 was truly outstanding. The final was won by a brilliant Spanish team before a full house of 100 000 at the Nou Camp, but the Australian team also covered itself in glory. The inaugural Olyroos boasted such prodigious talents as Mark Bosnich, Paul Okon and Ned Zelic, and but for the surprising decision of coach Eddie Thomson to reshape his team for the third/fourth play-off against Ghana, Australia could well have returned home with a bronze medal. Despite the 'advantage' of being able to include three over-age players for the 1996 Olympics, the Olyroos never looked like emulating that feat. But the Australians did manage the distinction of leading the defending champions, Spain, by two goals in a second round match in Orlando, only to be eliminated 3–2 in a heartbreaking finale.

It adds up to a rich heritage for the under-23 team, which in 2000 will be coached by Raul Blanco. And, once again, he has no shortage of talent at his disposal. In the embryonic stages of the preparation, Blanco chose largely to overlook his overseas-based contenders, and yet the squad still contained exciting prospects such as Brett Emerton, Clayton Zane, Jason Culina, Bill Damianos and Vince Grella. Once the going gets serious, expect the foreign legion—among them Ante Seric, Tynan Scope, Chris Coyne, Harry Kewell, Nick Rizzo, Hayden Foxe, Danny Milosevic, Ralph Bove, Lucas Neill and Andrew McDermott—to become fully involved. Nothing less than a medal at Sydney 2000 will satisfy the ambitions of the nation, of Blanco and of his players. And with the advantage of home support

ALL IS NOT LOST

(the Olyroos are likely to play their group matches before capacity crowds at the Sydney Football Stadium) a medal is certainly not beyond reach. Undoubtedly, it is a unique opportunity for the Olyroos, and one they can't afford to let slip.

Ultimately, however, the long-term health of the game cannot be entirely judged by the performance of Australia's national teams, at whatever level. While enormous goodwill can be generated by positive international results, history has shown that the feel-good factor does not last. The legacy of these results is what really counts. And in that context, only the premier domestic competition, the national league (NSL), can provide an enduring indication of the game's welfare. Only when the NSL develops into a thriving, exciting, professional competition will the game's future be secured.

The aim, certainly, has been embraced by Soccer Australia. Since taking office, Hill has made a priority of trying to revamp the NSL which, despite being the first national competition in any sport (established 1977) had clearly lost its way by the early 1990s. Hill was elected with a mandate to revitalise the league, and it is a task he has attacked with some gusto. In recent years he has sought to dilute the ethnic foundation of the league, a heritage proudly displayed by some of the country's most famous clubs. 'Mainstreaming' became the vogue word as Hill's administration set about dismantling the traditional power base and replacing it with centralised decision-making. As a result, Soccer Australia was able to dump ethnic-based clubs such as Parramatta Eagles, Heidelberg United and Brunswick Zebras, and replace them with broadly supported teams from key markets in Newcastle, Canberra and Perth.

Soccer Australia also gave the go-ahead for major Australian football (AFL) and rugby league clubs to invest in soccer teams as a way of utilising expensive facilities all year round. The reforms were welcomed at the time, but the truth is they have not always worked. Collingwood Warriors, an arm of the Collingwood AFL club, lasted less than a season in a severe embarrassment for Hill. But at least another Melbourne club with AFL connections, Carlton, has shown encouraging signs of lasting the distance. The jury remains out on the involvement of rugby league clubs, with Eastern Suburbs and Canterbury having nibbled at the edges of the sport by expressing interest in Sydney Olympic and Sydney United respectively. Time will tell whether this interest will manifest into something more concrete.

From the developing centres, only Perth Glory can claim to have made a serious impact. While Newcastle Breakers and Canberra Cosmos have struggled for money and support, the Glory have quickly emerged as the new benchmark of Australian soccer, smashing attendance records with an average of 11 600 in their debut season, increasing to 14 900 the following season, and generating huge media coverage in their home town. The privately backed Glory franchise represents the epitome of the brave new world espoused by Hill—a well-capitalised, broad-based, market-driven club which can help fulfil the ultimate dream of a fully-professional NSL by 2001.

That dream is enshrined in a five-year plan first formulated by Soccer Australia at a seminar in Wollongong midway through 1997. At that stage, of course, the Socceroos were still alive in World Cup terms, and optimism abounded. The game believed it was set to explode on the back of a successful France 98 campaign. It didn't happen, of course, and for the 1997–98 season crowds slumped appreciably.

There is no doubt that following the failure at the MCG, the targets have become more difficult to achieve. Yet if the upsurge in interest from the investment community is any guide, the long-term goal of a financially viable NSL may not be such a pipedream. In the early 1990s, when public and corporate interest in the NSL had plateaued, there was not a single club founded on private ownership. But by the time the NSL celebrated its 20th birthday in 1997, six clubs (Newcastle, Canberra, Wollongong, Perth, Carlton and Sydney Olympic) had either become privately owned or were investigating a change in structure. By the start of 1998, three more clubs (Brisbane Strikers, Sydney United and Adelaide City) were preparing to follow suit, while a consortium of Australian and Malaysian investors was backing the keenly awaited entry of Northern Spirit. Certainly private investment represents the way forward for a competition that has historically been under-capitalised. That has been recognised by consortiums from Townsville, Auckland, and the eastern suburbs of both Sydney and Melbourne, all of whom are keen to join the NSL by the turn of the century. The traditional membership-based clubs which do not heed the warning signs will, inevitably, have to make way.

Such a vision, certainly, is the centrepiece of Soccer Australia's strategic planning. Full-time professionalism is regarded as the panacea for the game's fundamental ill—the loss of so many players overseas. The argument goes that if players can earn a decent wage in the NSL, many of them will forget about going abroad. Certainly the presence of more than 80 Australians outside the country has seriously weakened the standard of the national league.

This thinking has been reinforced in a blueprint for the game's future commissioned by Soccer Australia and prepared by former president Sir Arthur

ALL IS NOT LOST

George. Sir Arthur argues that the costs of turning players from part-time to full-time are not as daunting as some might believe. And to assist clubs to pave the way for professionalism, his task force has recommended that the changeover be implemented gradually—from 10 players per club in 1998 to 16 players per club (plus four trainees) by season 2001–2. Other key recommendations include a salary cap, a minimum of 10 and a maximum of 14 clubs, a fully franchised league possibly including company-owned teams, AIS graduates being contracted by Soccer Australia for a period of three years to keep them in the NSL, and exploring previously untapped markets in Asia, Africa, Central America and Oceania to recruit affordable imports and thereby improve the quality of the league. While some of the ideas are not new, they remain as relevant as ever. And they dovetail with the aspirations of Soccer Australia. The hard part will be for the clubs to find the funds to implement them.

In the short term, at least, the money to pay for these grand visions will come from a private sector that has been swayed by the platform of reform being pushed by Soccer Australia. Television ratings are not yet at the level where serious income can be derived from rights fees. So for now, the business community is picking up the slack. But these investors will only persevere if the league proves itself a viable enterprise—essentially by earning worthwhile commercial television exposure and regularly attracting crowds of between 10 000 and 15 000. And in an increasingly competitive and saturated marketplace, where even well-funded sports like rugby league are struggling to attract an audience, that will be an achievement worth savouring.

Critically, a thriving national league would finally provide Australian soccer with the foundation to be able to fully explore its potential internationally. The world's strongest soccer nations all boast a healthy and dynamic domestic competition. Australia's soccer culture needs to emulate clubs such as Real Madrid, Manchester United and Ajax Amsterdam, all of which excite and sustain interest both locally and globally. Historically, Australia's place has been among the backmarkers. Hence the snide comments of the British journalists who likened Terry Venables taking on the Australian job as soccer's equivalent of running the Jamaican bobsleigh team. The jokes, of course, are hopelessly outdated, but they reflect a common international perception that Australia has not yet earned the right to be taken seriously. Those views, however narrow-minded, will be difficult to change.

But from those with a more receptive mind, due recognition has already arrived. After a decade of genuine progress at international level, supported by a world-class development system crowned by the Australian Institute of Sport, there is a consensus that Australian soccer stands on the precipice. But what, exactly, is beyond the horizon?

Globally, soccer is bigger than it has ever been before. It is virtually unrecognisable from the sport that entered the last decade of the 20th century. Most of the impetus has come from television.

In 1997, more than 800 internationals were played—the most in a single year since the first match was played between England and Scotland in 1872, and twice the amount of just five years earlier. Obviously, a large percentage of the fixtures were qualifiers for France 98, the break-up of the Soviet Union and various states in Eastern Europe precipitating a substantial increase in the number of participating nations. Yet many other fixtures, and tournaments, were especially created for the benefit of television. The advent of pay television, with its voracious need for 'product', has provided the catalyst. The impending arrival of digital television will only serve to increase the demand.

To justify those demands, and lay the groundwork for pay-per-view, the television networks have been prepared to fork out. In 1997, president Joao Havelange estimated FIFA's reserves at $6.2 billion—and this for an organisation that had been virtually bankrupt 20 years before. Most of the money has been generated by television rights, and the sponsorship dollars that follow the small screen. To emphasise just how big soccer has become, Havelange suggested that the sport was set to enter the new century as a $150 billion per year industry, involving 400 million people either directly or indirectly.

Little wonder, then, that soccer enjoys a global position of commercial privilege and power. And the best players are being remunerated accordingly. The landmark Bosman case in Europe, in which players won greater autonomy and freedom of movement, slowed the wholesale use of transfer fees. But clubs have responded by locking players into long-term contracts. If they seek transfer during contract they still command a premium. In 1997 Ronaldo transferred from Barcelona to Inter Milan for $69 million, while his fellow Brazilian Denilson shifted from Sao Paulo to Real Betis in Spain for $55.2 million. Staggering sums, certainly, and a clear indication that soccer's future is now firmly entwined with big business.

At the same time, clubs are rewarding their most valued players with wages of up to $100 000 per week. According to one international marketing and management company, the average salary in Europe has grown to around $700 000 per season—and that does not include match payments and bonuses. In turn, the workload for players is threatening to spiral out of control. The creation of a fixed, coordinated international calendar has been a dream of FIFA for a number of years. That is the way, it is claimed, to protect the best players from burnout and to ensure the marketplace is not saturated with useless tournaments and meaningless games. And yet the same FIFA executives have granted official status to the Confederations Cup and are now talking enthusiastically of a world club challenge. These matches are of huge benefit to developing countries like Australia, but in the established nations they only serve to escalate the age-old club versus country dispute. The big European clubs who are paying their top foreigners huge amounts of money are not happy that they have to continually release them for FIFA tournaments—apart from the World Cup and the Olympics. A major showdown, perhaps in the courts, is looming.

The ultimate challenge for everyone connected with the sport of soccer as it approaches the new century is to understand the scale, and the scope, of what it has become. Most of the change has been caused by money. In Europe, stock market flotations are in vogue, with many clubs casting envious eyes at Manchester United, who floated in 1991 and now has a turnover of $120 million. The trend which began in England has extended to Italy, Germany, France and Spain, with South America and even Africa (Zambian club Mulfulira Wanderers are planning an entry on the Lusaka stock exchange) getting in on the act.

Clubs see public share issues as the quickest way to earn the cash needed to pay for the exploding wages and transfer fees of the post-Bosman era. Another key development is the growing involvement of those institutional investors who have been smart enough to recognise the potential profitability of the game. Britain's richest man, the reclusive Joe Lewis, heads a company called ENIC which is expected to either partly or wholly own eight different clubs in eight different European countries by 1999. It is only a matter of time before like-minded consortiums follow suit, much like the traditional multinationals who scour the world to create a network of investments. Taken a step further, it will not be long before the big European clubs, flush with funds from pay television or the share issues, buy smaller clubs to create nurseries of talent. Players who can be signed for next to nothing and then sold off for millions are a valuable commodity indeed. In Australia, the process has already begun, with English club West Ham recently investing in two state league clubs, Blacktown City (NSW) and Kingsway Olympic (Western Australia), for precisely that purpose.

Globally, the big winners from these rapid changes will be the players, the directors and investors, and the pay television networks who are able to secure subscribers to the world's most popular product. The big loser, unquestionably, will be the average fan, who either through merchandise, ticket prices or television subscription fees will have to pay for all of this.

Australia's place in this increasingly complex football world remains uncertain. It will take time for the local game to fully digest the implications. But the benefit of that breathing space is that Australian soccer can step back and decide which changes are beneficial and which are not. Given its chequered history, it should be capable of learning from any mistakes.

APPENDIX
THE MATCHES

GAME ONE
FOUR NATIONS SERIES
Australia v New Zealand
SCORE: 1–0
SCORER: Matthew Bingley
VENUE: Lakeside Stadium, Melbourne
CROWD: 10 500
TEAM: Kalac; Bingley, Tobin (Longo 76), Ivanovic, Genc (Casserly 12); Foster, Hooker (Enes 66); Trimboli (Tapai 66); Zdrilic, Trajanovski (Spink 82).

GAME TWO
FOUR NATIONS SERIES
Australia v South Korea
SCORE: 2–1
SCORERS: Bingley, Edwards
VENUE: Lang Park, Brisbane
CROWD: 15 161
TEAM: Kalac; Bingley (Trajkovski 92), Tobin, Ivanovic, Babic, Hooker; Foster, Enes (Edwards 70); Trimboli (Spink 78); Zdrilic, Trajanovski (Tapai 67).

GAME THREE
FOUR NATIONS SERIES
Australia v Norway
SCORE: 1–0
SCORER: Hooker
VENUE: Sydney Football Stadium
CROWD: 17 429
TEAM: Kalac; Bingley, Tobin, Ivanovic, Babic, Hooker; Foster, Enes; Trimboli (Spink 71); Trajanovski (Tapai 69), Zdrilic.

GAME FOUR
FOUR NATIONS SERIES
Macedonia v Australia
SCORE: 1–0
SCORER: A. Vidmar
VENUE: Gradski Stadium, Skopje
CROWD: 9000
TEAM: Bosnich; Durakovic, T. Vidmar, Kulcsar, Horvat, Slater; Corica (Skoko 70), Zelic (Mori 64), A. Vidmar; Viduka, Aloisi (Tiatto 61).

GAME FIVE
FRIENDLY
Hungary v Australia
SCORE: 3–1
SCORERS: A Vidmar 2, Muscat
VENUE: Nepstadium, Budapest
CROWD: 20 000
TEAM: Filan; Slater, T. Vidmar, Popovic, Horvat, Lazaridis; Skoko (Muscat 46), Zelic, A. Vidmar; Arnold (Aloisi 78), Viduka.

GAME SIX
WORLD CUP
Australia v Solomon Islands
SCORE: 13–0
SCORERS: Mori 5, Aloisi 5, Bosnich, Tapai, Foster
VENUE: Parramatta Stadium, Sydney
CROWD: 3127
TEAM: Bosnich; Slater (Tapai 70), Tobin, T. Vidmar, Horvat, Lazardis (Hooker 73); Foster, Zelic, A. Vidmar; Mori, Aloisi.

/167

GAME SEVEN
WORLD CUP
Australia v Tahiti
SCORE: 5–0
SCORERS: Trimboli 2, Arnold, A. Vidmar, Bingley
VENUE: Parramatta Stadium, Sydney
CROWD: 2869
Team: Kalac; Bingley (Tapai 70), Muscat, Moore, Ivanovic, Hooker (Lazaridis 70); Enes, Zelic, A. Vidmar (Trajanovski 46); Arnold, Trimboli.

GAME EIGHT
WORLD CUP
Australia v Solomon Islands
SCORE: 6–2
SCORERS: Tapai 2, Arnold, Slater, A. Vidmar, own goal
VENUE: Parramatta Stadium, Sydney
CROWD: 2122
TEAM: Petkovic; Tapai (Muscat 67), Tobin, T. Vidmar, Ivanovic, Lazardis; Slater, Enes (Trajanovski 75), Skoko (A. Vidmar 67), Mori.

GAME NINE
WORLD CUP
Australia v Tahiti
Score: 2–0
SCORERS: Trimboli, Zelic
VENUE: Parramatta Stadium, Sydney
CROWD: 2918
TEAM: Bosnich; Bingley (Trajanovski 78), Moore, (Tobin 46), Popovic, Horvat, Hooker; Foster, Zelic, A Vidmar; Mori (Trimboli 78), Aloisi.

GAME TEN
WORLD CUP
New Zealand v Australia
SCORE: 3–0
SCORERS: Aloisi, A. Vidmar, Foster
VENUE: North Harbour Stadium, Auckland
CROWD: 23 000
TEAM: Bosnich; Slater, Ivanokvic, Tobin (c), Moore (T. Vidmar 87), Lazaridis; Foster, Zelic, A. Vidmar; Arnold, Aloisi.

GAME ELEVEN
WORLD CUP
Australia v New Zealand
SCORE: 2–0
SCORERS: Zelic, Arnold
VENUE: Parramatta Stadium, Sydney
CROWD: 14 045
TEAM: Bosnich; Slater, Ivanokvic, Tobin (c), Moore (T Vidmar 34), Lazaridis; Foster, Zelic, A. Vidmar; Arnold (Trimboli 79), Aloisi (Mori 86).

GAME TWELVE
FRIENDLY
Tunisia v Australia
SCORE: 3–0
SCORERS: A. Vidmar, Viduka, Bingley
VENUE: El Menzah Stadium, Tunis
CROWD: 15 000
TEAM: Kalac; Muscat, Ivanovic, Tobin (c), T. Vidmar, Hooker (Trimboli 86); Skok (Bingley 66), Zelic, A. Vidmar (Slater 55); Aloisi (Kewell 46), Viduka (Mori 86).

M/A/T/C/H/E/S

GAME THIRTEEN
WORLD CUP
Iran v Australia
SCORE: 1–1
SCORER: Kewell
VENUE: Azadi Stadium, Tehran
CROWD: 128 000
TEAM: Bosnich; Slater (Tapai 56), Tobin (c), Moore, Horvat, T. Vidmar; Foster, Zelic, A. Vidmar (Lazaridis 56); Viduka, Kewell (Arnold 86).

GAME FOURTEEN
WORLD CUP
Australia v Iran
SCORE: 2–2
SCORERS: A. Vidmar, Kewell
VENUE: Melbourne Cricket Ground
CROWD: 85 022*
TEAM: Bosnich; Slater (T. Vidmar 81), Tobin (c), Moore (Arnold 86), Horvat, Lazaridis; A. Vidmar (Tapai 81), Zelic, Foster; Viduka, Kewell.
*Australian record

GAME FIFTEEN
CONFEDERATIONS CUP
Australia v Mexico
SCORE: 3–1
SCORERS: Viduka, Aloisi, Mori
VENUE: King Fahd Stadium, Riyadh
CROWD: 15 000
TEAM: Kalac; Slater (Tapai 81), Tobin (c), Horvat, T. Vidmar, Lazaridis; A. Vidmar (Hooker 46), Zelic, Foster; Viduka (Mori 73), Aloisi.

GAME SIXTEEN
CONFEDERATIONS CUP
Australia v Brazil
SCORE: 0–0
SCORERS: Viduka, Aloisi, Mori
VENUE: King Fahd Stadium, Riyadh
CROWD: 11 000
TEAM: Bosnich; T. Vidmar, Horvat, Tobin (c), Ivanovic, Lazaridis; A. Vidmar (Tapai 59), Foster, Zelic; Viduka (Bingley 92), Aloisi (Mori 69).

GAME SEVENTEEN
CONFEDERATIONS CUP
Saudi Arabia v Australia
SCORE: 0–1
VENUE: King Fahd Stadium, Riyadh
CROWD: 20 000
TEAM: Bosnich; Slater, Horvat, Tobin (c), Ivanovic, Lazaridis; Skoko (A. Vidmar 74), Foster, Zelic; Mori (Kewell 66), Aloisi (Viduka 66).

GAME EIGHTEEN
CONFEDERATIONS CUP
(Semifinal)
Australia v Uruguay
SCORE: 1–0
SCORER: Kewell
VENUE: King Fahd Stadium, Riyadh
CROWD: 22 000
TEAM: Bosnich; Muscat, Tobin (c), Ivanovic, T. Vidmar, Lazaridis; A. Vidmar (Skoko 82), Foster, Zelic; Viduka, Kewell.

GAME NINETEEN
CONFEDERATIONS CUP
(Final)
Australia v Brazil
Score: 0–6
Venue: King Fahd Stadium, Riyadh
Crowd: 40 000
Team: Bosnich; T. Vidmar (Muscat 30), Ivanovic, Tobin (c), Horvat (Bingley 56), Lazaridis; A. Vidmar (Aloisi 30), Foster, Zelic; Viduka, Kewell.

GAME TWENTY
OPTUS WORLD SERIES
Australia v Chile
Score: 0–1
Venue: Olympic Park, Melbourne
Crowd: 12 000
Team: Kalac; de Amicis (Lozanovski 46), Tobin (c), Horvat, Hooker; Mendez (Trajanovski 63), Bilokapic (Halpin 46), Tapai (Emerton 75); Markovski, Trimboli (Saad 63).

GAME TWENTY-ONE
OPTUS WORLD SERIES
Australia v South Korea
Score: 1–0
Scorer: Tapai
Venue: Sydney Football Stadium
Crowd: 9823
Team: J. Petkovic; Emerton, Tobin (c), M. Babic, Horvat, de Amicis; Tapai, Halpin, Trajanovski (Mendez 72); Saad (Bilokapic 91), Trimboli (Markovski 72).

GAME TWENTY-TWO
OPTUS WORLD SERIES
Australia v Japan
Score: 0–3
Scorer: Tapai
Venue: Hindmarsh Stadium, Adelaide
Crowd: 9300
Team: Kalac; Emerton, Tobin, Ivanovic (c), Longo (Horvat 46), de Amicis; Tapai (Lozanovski 83), Halpin, Trajanovski; Markovski (Mendez 46 [Trimboli 63]), Saad.